THE
HOMESTEADER
MINDSET

BUILD A SUSTAINABLE LIFE
WHEREVER YOU ARE

ELIZABETH BRUCKNER

The
Homesteader
Mindset

Build A Sustainable Life
Wherever You Are

Elizabeth Bruckner

Published by Deep Forest Company

Cover and interior designed by Dino Marino Design

Paperback ISBN: 979-8-9885278-1-7

DEEP FOREST

YOU'RE INVITED!

Hello, friend,

Community is essential to a homesteader mindset. And for that reason, I would love to deepen our connection. I have many things to share with you. If I shared them all right here, this book would be way too heavy to carry.

You are cordially invited to download the book bonuses that I mention throughout this book.

I've created a free resource guide for readers who are interested in taking a deep dive into the connected way of life. It's my gift to you!

Plus, we'll get to know each other, which is nice. You'll be the first to know about events. You'll even receive updates on my upcoming books.

Visit: www.createwellnessproject.com/bookbonus.

Thank you for picking up my book. Your time is extremely valuable, and I'm grateful you chose to spend some of it with me.

All the best,

Elizabeth

TABLE OF CONTENTS

PART ONE

WHAT IS A HOMESTEADER MINDSET?

What if you woke up every single morning with something to look forward to? Imagine a day where you are not only present but also find pleasure in the little moments. Remember that delicious feeling of sleep after a long day of playing in the sun as a child?

That's still available to you. A homesteader mindset will feel different for each human, but one thing is common. You will use your mind and body each day in ways that make you feel more alive. You will be more a part of your community and more at peace. The ideas and actions detailed in this book are here to provide you with multiple mindset shifts. Today, we are flipping the switch.

Humans learn best through story. In part one of this book, you'll meet our heroes and heroines: Sara, Jim, Tamara, Mitch, and Lucy. We'll walk with them throughout the book. They will show us how they transformed their existences into connected, vibrant lives.

Through their stories, I'll explain key concepts that you can incorporate immediately. Within the first few chapters, you can begin to transform your life. Small shifts make big waves in surprising and seemingly magical ways. Their stories will birth new ideas for you to try.

Part one of this book is an introduction to the concept of a homesteader mindset. You'll read accounts of how others created their tailor-made lifestyle. We lay all our cards on the table. You can pick and choose what your next adventure will be.

I invite you to use this book fully. Have a highlighter and pen handy—scribble in the margins—underline what speaks to you. Use the blank pages at the front and back of the book to jot down notes. Make this a living document. It's here to support you on your journey to a homesteader mindset.

CHAPTER 1

AT HOME WITH SARA & JIM

MIDDLE-CLASS SUBURBAN HOMESTEADING

Sara and Jim live in a bedroom community sixty miles outside of Columbus, Ohio. They have two school-aged children and a rescue dog. Jim works full-time as a phlebotomist and part-time as the family's breakfast chef. Sara works part-time as a social worker and full-time as captain of the house.

Let's look at what a homesteader mindset looks like for them.

Monday morning rush hour at their home starts early. Sara wakes up at 5:30 a.m. to give herself a mindful moment before the flurry of morning activity. Most days, she follows the *Miracle Morning* routine by Hal Elrod, but she's tweaked it a bit.

Sara washes her face and brushes her teeth while reciting a few personal intentions. If it's a fancy day, she'll put on a little makeup before getting dressed. Coconut oil mixed with essential oil of lavender is her deodorant.

She drinks a glass of garden herbal infusion and carries another glass to her favorite chair. (Check out the Recipe section of this book for more information on garden herbal infusions.)

She grabs her shoes and takes her dog for a twenty-minute walk. Exercise and fresh air lift her spirit. She allows herself a little time to daydream about her newest fun project, a small class she's leading. A group of friends want to learn how to dry basil and understand its medicinal properties.

Once back home, Sara begins her mindfulness routine. Her beverage is waiting for her as a reward for her exercise. She enjoys a ten-minute meditation followed by a reading from an inspirational book. She then journals for ten minutes.

By 6:30 a.m., the house is buzzing. The kiddos are brushing their teeth. Jim is making scrambled eggs for breakfast. Everyone sits at the table at 6:45 a.m. for breakfast together.

Jim and Sara decided that breakfast was the best way to keep their family connected. Lunch is usually at work or school, and dinner can be tricky at times. Their sixty-minute breakfast is a great way to catch up with each other on a regular basis. It's gratifying to start the day as a family.

Around 7:45 a.m., the kids clear the table and do the dishes. They add their food scraps to the kitchen scrap container in the freezer.

Mondays are the day of the week when Sara's thirteen-year-old son, Zach, cooks family dinner. He double-checks all the needed ingredients from their weekly market trip. He's looking forward to trying out a new recipe.

Sara spends fifteen minutes tending to the garden and the compost. She then puts their lunches and backpacks near the door. The four of them packed everything last night before their evening showers. Jim grabs his lunch, gives each member of his family a kiss goodbye, and sets off to work.

Their children are part of a homeschool co-op. Each family dedicates one day of the school week to teaching twelve children in the program. Sara drops the children off at Wendy's house for five hours of Spanish, math, writing, and woodshop.

The drive to Wendy's house offers another opportunity for Sara to connect with her children. There is a no-cell-phone rule in the car. Instead, they talk about what each of them is most looking forward to today. Her youngest son, Matthew, can't wait to have a chat in Spanish with his language exchange friend via Skype. Her eldest son, Zach, is intent on finishing his woodworking project.

After dropping them off, Sara drives to work in silence. Sometimes she listens to her favorite permaculture podcast. On other days, she sings along to her favorite playlist. Today, she chooses to be with her thoughts in silence. She has a busy day ahead, and allowing a little quiet time is a nice way to begin her work week.

What if you are not a morning person?

What if you don't homeschool your kids?

What if you don't know how to scramble eggs?

We will cover the road map to finding these answers and more in the chapters that follow. Right now, I want to show you examples of homesteader lives. As you are reading this, what piece sounds like it would be amazing if you could incorporate it into your day? Write that down. Right now. Grab a notebook. It doesn't need to be fancy.

Write "My Homesteader Mindset" at the top of the first page and answer the reflection questions as you read. When I use a journal for a book I'm reading, I put the page number of the book in each entry so I can refer to the description and questions.

You'll also want to write down questions as they come up. Either they will be answered later in the book, or you will need to take a poll and see whether anyone else has tips for you. We'll talk about polls in a bit.

Oftentimes, answers will come to you while reading this book. As you become clearer about your goals, your subconscious mind will start working for you. Solutions will pop up when you least expect them.

Whatever form the answer takes, it's necessary to write it down. That will create more space for taking in new information while you wait for your solution. A great book about how the mind operates is *Your Brain at Work* by David Rock. He suggests keeping the mind (or the stage, as he calls it) free of clutter. Writing things down is an effective way to do this.

Your first reflection for your journal is "What pieces of this story resonate with me? What part of Sara and Jim's life would I like?" Free your mind of limiting thoughts. We're talking about the sky's the limit here.

Suppose you had a billion dollars—a miracle happened while you were sleeping—and you had unlimited time. What chunk of this story would you like to be yours? Write out a few sentences about what that would look like for you. Seeing it is the first step to bringing those possibilities to you.

Allowing yourself to see the desired result without getting bogged down in the how is a skill worth acquiring. Suspend your disbelief for the duration of this book. At the very worst, you'll stay exactly where you are. But even one slight shift could change your life. It happens all the time.

Let's answer one question that might have popped up. What does "take a poll" mean? Taking a poll is when you have a question, find people who seem to have what you want in relation to that question. Then ask them how they got it.

Here's an example. I'm currently working on shifting my mindset around wealth. For most of my life, I considered money a dirty thing. I wanted nothing to do with it. In return, money didn't want much to do with me. Once I decided to shift my money mindset, I asked people questions about wealth. I chose people who seemed to have a healthy relationship with money. I wanted to see what they were doing and how they were thinking differently than me.

The same is true for homesteading. Perhaps you are not sure how on earth you're going to be able to start a morning routine by prepping in the evening. Ask your friends who seem to have a peaceful morning routine. What does their system look like? How did they get started? Was it their dad who taught them organization? Is it possible for you to chat with their dad?

Start with people you know in person and work your way outward. I'm a big fan of online communities, but they are lacking in many ways. Someone's Instagram feed might not be a great snapshot of what their lives are like.

I know a few well-known influencers. There are aspects of their lives that I would never want for myself. If I knew them solely from their public persona, I would imagine they had exactly what I wanted. Same goes for celebrities. What you see is not always what you get. Find your role models in real life. The less photoshopping, the better.

At Sara and Jim's house, the children play an active role in the household. They have chores and responsibilities like cooking dinner once a week. This makes the family more of a team. It allows for creative expression and takes the heavy lifting off mom and dad.

It wasn't always like this for Sara and Jim. For years, both parents worked fifty or more hours per week. They didn't see their children as much as they would have liked. When they did spend time with them, it was usually while shuffling them from home to school or daycare. Sara nearly forgot the color of her eldest son's eyes because they were constantly riveted on the happenings of his cell phone.

Jim and Sara both wanted to work less, but they could barely pay the bills. For them to change, there needed to be a serious wake-up call. They got one in the way of a terrible event. Sara was involved in a car accident that left her bedridden for several months.

Suddenly, they had to do without a second income. They looked through their budget and cut out whatever expenses they could. They started working on ways to lower their monthly nut.

There was a transition time in Sara's recovery when she was well enough to putter around the house for an hour. Still, she was not yet strong enough to go back to work. She started learning how to cook one-pot meals like chili and chicken soup. Before that, the family ate processed food and takeout.

Saving money was a priority during her recovery. Cooking whole food meals was nourishing for their bodies, and it was also healthy for their pocketbook. She went a step further with saving cash.

When she realized how expensive herbs were, she considered trying to grow a few. As it turns out, herbs are often the gateway plant for gardeners. Chives, mint, and oregano grew without much effort.

Her mindset switch happened when she began to get curious. What if growing and cooking whole foods became an adventure for her family? Why was oregano so important in Italian sauces? What do modern researchers say about its antiviral, antibacterial properties?

When she needed to rest her body, she would crawl into bed and watch a video about permaculture. That's where she learned that growing food like nature does is one of the easiest ways to garden. There is a list of recommendations for permaculture resources in your online book bonus guide. Visit: www.createwellnessproject.com/bookbonus.

Jim was relieved to see Sara's recovery continue. He had been worried that her injuries would cause her to spiral into depression. Instead, she found ways to keep herself occupied. And happy bonus! Sara's new hobby of traditional, easy cooking was bringing the family closer.

Jim's mindset shift occurred when he noticed that his sons were well more often than sick. He intuitively knew this had something to do with nutritious food. Sara had replaced the takeout processed food they had been consuming with real food. The one-pot meals that Sara was cooking up were mouthwatering. He couldn't wait to come home to enjoy dinner with his family.

Sara was invigorated by her daily discoveries. She learned to make household cleaners from ingredients like vinegar and essential oils. For some, essential oils might be too strong. Vinegar cleans windows and counters just as well without fragrance.

One day, Jim was utterly confused. He couldn't understand why their office smelled like a salad. As it turns out, Sarah had used vinegar mixed with a few drops of oregano oil to clean the desk. Once he saw her with a cloth and spray bottle in hand, it all made sense.

Every day brought new and sometimes humorous stories into their home.

When Sara was well enough to go back to work, the two of them sat down and talked about what that would look like. Sara found a new sense of fulfillment. Feeding her family with food she grew in their small suburban garden was a big part of her life now. Fresh vegetables from her garden had more nutritional qualities than store-bought vegetables. Food was becoming their family's first line of defense.

Another gift that Sara's being home brought them was things were more stable at home. If something broke, Sara was able to fix it or get it fixed in a matter of weeks, not years. She was more available for their kids during the day and had a better pulse on what they were learning at school. The organization of their days seemed a bit more streamlined. They had time and energy to chat about what they wanted their lives to look like.

Finally, there was a little more breathing room.

Together they came up with a plan. Sara would return to work part-time, and Jim would rework his schedule to cap his full-time job at forty hours per week.

They decided to downsize to a smaller house in a less expensive part of town. Their front yard was mostly lawn with a concrete backyard, but it was better than going into debt. Sara immediately started container gardening in the backyard to reduce their grocery bill.

With a little more space in their schedules, they started having family meetings. They discussed how best to reconnect as a team. The boys had chores before this shift, but they were mostly tasks without a lot of freedom.

When Jim suggested each son take charge of dinner once per week, he was surprised at their enthusiasm. The first few weeks were all about recreating their favorite fast-food meals. Jim and Sara offered very little guidance on how to do it. The parents merely requested that the meals consist of whole foods and a side of vegetables. Over time, the task grew into curiosity about what new meals the boys could create.

Zach had been bitten by the foodie bug. He planned his weekly meal a few days before shopping day. He was enamored with an eighty-year-old Italian chef on YouTube. His meals are relatively simple to make but go far beyond anything his parents have ever learned to cook.

On Friday afternoons, the boys accompany Sara to the grocery store. Each member of the family is equipped with a separate list of items to find. This cuts their shopping time down and teaches the boys how to organize their food planning. Sara and Jim have a clear goal. They want their boys to grow up knowing how to be adults.

After dropping the food off at the house, the three of them celebrate. Shopping is followed by a weekly trip to the park for a wander with their dog. Sometimes, the boys' friends or one of Sara's buddies will join them for the grocery-to-green excursion. Often, Jim meets them there after work. Having a set time for walking in nature is an easy way to de-stress and also be available for friends who want to chat.

As for the big change to a homeschooling co-op, that didn't arrive until two years into their journey. Each change happened organically. One piece at a time fits nicely into the landscape of their lives. We'll talk more about how to puzzle together the life you desire in part four of this book.

EASY-BREEZY END OF CHAPTER TASKS

- Create a Homesteader Mindset Journal. This can be as simple as grabbing a ninety-nine-cent spiral notebook. Or as fancy as buying one at that swanky gift shop you always walk by. Or as artsy as cutting up some magazine images and gluing them to the cover of a composition notebook. On the first page, write the title of this book. That's it. Your first task is complete!

- What slices of this story resonate with you? Take five minutes to write a few sentences in your Homesteader Mindset Journal. What would those characteristics look like in your life? Allow yourself childlike optimism.

- Write a few sentences about how it feels to imagine the good life you wrote about in the second question. If they are pleasant feelings, enjoy them. Relish them. If a few unpleasant emotions pop up, make space for them. Everyone gets a seat at the table here. In our chapter on tools, you'll have actions you can take to process negativity. For now, express your thoughts without judgment.

CHAPTER 2

TAMARA'S ADVENTURE

WORKING POOR CITY HOMESTEADING

Tamara is a twenty-five-year-old barista who shares a two-bedroom apartment with roommates. They live together in the bustling city of Houston, Texas. She has limited disposable income as city living is expensive. Oftentimes, she will describe herself as creatively rich. Tamara has found ways to work around a low-paying job and high rent.

Her apartment has no outdoor space for her garden. Yet she's found ways to grow her own food without the expense of renting land. Two of her talents are inventive problem-solving and tenacity. She moved to Houston from a small town with $700 in her pocket.

Though she grew up in a rural area, her family didn't grow food on their land. They commuted to work every day, ate mostly processed food, and didn't get much rest. Tamara felt she wanted something different for her future, but she wasn't sure what. When a friend told her about the two years he spent in Houston, she decided to move there.

She stayed with family friends for two weeks while she got a job at the nearby coffeehouse and found a room for rent. The first few months were difficult for her. She was homesick. She missed her family and friends, and asked herself again and again, "Why am I doing this?"

Her roommates were nice. They would invite her to social gatherings, but there wasn't a lot of common interest. To be fair, Tamara didn't *have* a lot of interests.

If she was being honest, she could see that a lot of her free time was spent watching TV shows. The characters made up for the friends she didn't yet have in her new city. She knew she needed to step out of her comfort zone but wasn't sure how.

Here's a great place to stop and reflect. Please take out your journal and scribble down a few things that eat up your time. I'm not talking about things that make you feel good. For instance, a five-minute rescue dog success video is not going to make me a million dollars. But it is a great way to open the hope valve in my heart when I'm feeling down.

On the flip side, watching TV for three hours when there are other tasks that will bring me connection is not quality time, and neither is getting sucked into news stories. It happens from time to time, but it never, ever leaves me feeling like I've used my time and energy wisely.

What are your sand traps? What is promising you a connection but giving you mud instead? Write it down. Get it out. That's how it will begin to change.

Okay, back to Tamara's journey.

She visited the library and took out every single book she could find on happiness. That's what she wanted. So, why not start there? She found *Digital Minimalism* by Cal Newport to be a game changer. She started cutting down on her TV, phone, and internet usage by spending more time exploring the city. After all, walking was free.

During one of her morning strolls, she noticed a farmers' market near her apartment. It was the first city farmers' market she had ever visited and she was in love. The smells of food trucks filled her nostrils. Small children playing tag in between their parents gave her a smile.

Her eyes were met with bright-colored vegetables she didn't even know existed. She couldn't get over the varieties of purple carrots that were being sold. And the radishes that looked like peppermint candy dazzled her. So many new things to explore. She decided to splurge on a two-dollar bundle of fresh herbs. And thus, her weekly visit to the farmers' market became her ritual.

After the market, she returned home and divided her aromatic prize into two bundles. One bundle would go directly into a vase on her bedroom windowsill. Whenever she walked by the window, she would stop and take in the scent of her bouquet. She called it her herbal vacation. Her favorite herbs for the windowsill were basil and lavender.

The other bundle would be washed and put in a clear pitcher. She would fill the pitcher with water and leave it next to the vase on the windowsill. In a few hours, she had herbal-infused water that made her feel like she was visiting a posh spa.

Week after week, she enjoyed her herbal excursions. They offered her a small taste of the lush green that she missed from her hometown. One morning, Tamara was chatting with one of her regular customers, Ester, and was waxing poetic about her herbal vacations.

Ester asked Tamara why she had never considered growing herbs. "Oh, I could never do that. I don't have any outside space to grow things." Ester explained that Tamara could try growing basil on her windowsill.

What a novel idea! Tamara began watching YouTube videos about how to grow plants on a windowsill. From there, she ventured into videos about the medicinal properties of basil. A little bit further down the rabbit hole had her looking up herbs that she could grow that would help her anxiety. Lemon balm is well known for helping calm nerves. She started adding that to her herbal infusions.

Before long, she had a beautiful wish list of plants and not enough window space. Ester and other customers would ask Tamara how her windowsill garden was going. She'd share about how pretty her basil looked every morning. She even ventured into growing sweet potatoes as a vine houseplant.

Little discoveries excited her. For example, she had no idea that she could eat sweet potato greens. So, that heart-shaped leaf houseplant was regularly trimmed and cooked up in a sauté. The more she grew, the more she wanted to prepare meals with her fresh food. She'd found a hobby that gave her joy.

This went on for a few months until she woke up one day with an inspired thought. "I don't have a yard, but others do. What if I grew food in someone else's yard?" She couldn't wait to talk with Ester about this.

As it turns out, Ester's neighbor, Bao, was having health issues that made it impossible for her to keep up her garden. She asked Bao if she'd be interested in sharing her garden space with Tamara. As rent, Tamara would give Bao half of the produce from the garden.

Reflection time again, my reader friends. If you don't currently have access to land, but you fancy growing food, what are some ways you could find space? If you are lacking in other material that will help you obtain more connection, use that object as your goal.

I usually find my opportunities through reverse engineering. Years ago, I needed to obtain a treadmill to exercise my foster dog. As a graduate school student, I didn't have the funds to buy one. I found one on Freecycle, but it wasn't by waiting for one to pop up.

Usually, items like that are snatched up by people who are way more connected to their laptops than I am. Instead, I reverse engineered it. I wrote a short but compelling story about my foster rescue dog and put it as a wanted ad on Freecycle. Someone loved the idea of helping a rescue pup, and I was gifted with a working treadmill for free.

Word of caution. The object you think is going to make everything better doesn't always do that. My foster dog hated the treadmill. At the time, I had no idea how to do choice-based dog training, which would have gotten him accustomed to it. So, the treadmill was gifted a year later to another hopeful treadmill dreamer.

What are some ways you could reverse engineer a necessity for your homesteader mindset? Write down some ideas. If you get stuck, set a timer and spend five minutes searching for ideas online.

Let's return to Tamara.

The garden barter turned out to be a fine deal for everyone. Tamara now had room to grow herbs, vegetables, and even a few edible flowers. Before her afternoon shifts at the coffeehouse, she would walk over to her plot of land and tend to her garden. Sometimes, she would spend a quick fifteen minutes watering. Other times, she'd stay for an hour or so tinkering in the dappled morning sun.

One of her favorite things to do is sit on a wood stump, sip tea, and watch the bees dance from one flower to the next. She was surprised to learn that bees take naps in comfy blooms. Bao visits with her and shares in the bee-watching. They've developed a lasting friendship.

While chatting with a vendor at the farmers' market, Tamara learned that he didn't have room this season to grow basil. She had an abundance of it in her garden. It was then that she decided to start selling her herbs to vendors at the market.

She also started selling herbs to the coffeehouse. The café now offers herbal infusions on its drink menu. Hot peppermint infusion is a top seller.

Through her friendships at the coffeehouse and farmers' market, Tamara is well known in her neighborhood. People stop her on the street to ask her how her herb farm is going. She is delighted to feel like she belongs.

Her sales from the garden afford her one additional day off at the coffeehouse. She went from working five days a week to four days. She invested one of her days off into learning about regenerative farming practices. She asked a nearby permaculture farm whether they accepted volunteers. It is there that she is learning about designing land for water conservation. Stacking the functions of plants and animals is an important lesson, too.

What does stacking the functions mean? We'll get to that later in the book. I promise.

Tamara's life became more connected. She found an area of focus that brings her immense pleasure. Working the land is important to her. Deepening relationships with people in her community gives her a sense of purpose. She found a home in Houston.

EASY-BREEZY END OF CHAPTER TASKS

- Create a list of things that eat up your time without offering you much quality. What are your sand traps?
- Take that list and see whether you can tweak any of the actions to offer more quality.
  - TV is a waste of time for me, but I enjoy watching when I'm too tired to do anything else. I incorporate language learning into the habit. I only watch TV in Spanish or French.
  - If scrolling social media is your sand trap, add a quality behavior right before you check your feed. Watch a sixty-second video on something that you need to learn. Or do three sets of squats before you scroll.
- Make a list of things you do that provide connection. Maybe it's visiting your grandmother once a week and listening to her childhood stories. Perhaps it's going for a walk and noticing the seasonal changes in your neighborhood. If the activity gives you a sense of being grounded, write it down.
  - Schedule one of the things in your connection list once a day. If you only wrote down things that take hours to do, tailor them to fifteen minutes.
    - Maybe you can't visit your grandmother this week, but you can schedule a call with her on your way to work.
    - A walk in the neighborhood might be too difficult after a long day of work. A short stroll during lunch hour is a great way to sip fresh air.

CHAPTER 3

MITCH & LUCY FIND THEIR WAY

FIXED INCOME RURAL HOMESTEADING

Doing what needs to be done. That's what Lucy and Mitch call homesteading. It's saving money and being smart about their garbage. Their story explains the subtle changes that occurred as they began homesteading.

Lucy and Mitch are a retired couple living in a rural part of Pennsylvania. They've never called themselves homesteaders. They don't give talks on how to live authentically. All that seems a bit too much for this couple. They would say that their homesteader mindset journey started as a fun jobby.

Job + Hobby = Jobby

Before starting their garden, Mitch was feeling despondent about retired life. He used to work long hours and brainstorm with his colleagues. There wasn't much to do during his leisure years. Because he and his wife live on a fixed income, there's not a lot of wiggle room for investing. So, he needed a business that wouldn't cost much money.

Living in a rural area, their property was spacious but undeveloped. It wouldn't cost much to buy some seeds. Ever the entrepreneur, Mitch decided to start a market garden. A market garden is a garden that grows food for selling to others.

After forty years of being best friends as well as husband and wife, Lucy enjoys hanging out with Mitch. So, the two retirees enrolled in a beginner gardening class at the local community college. Initially, it wasn't a hobby; it was a way to create extra income.

Their grandson helped them clear a small patch of lawn outside the kitchen for their first garden. Mitch would watch to see who visited and reported it to Lucy as she made their morning coffee. For the first time in his seventy years, he began to notice the vivid colors of backyard birds. He took an interest in wildlife habits. Mitch's daughter bought him an audiobook about birds of Pennsylvania.

As time went on, a beautiful relationship developed between the humans and the garden. Lucy began to wake up early to check on her babies. That's what she called her seedlings. She was excited to see which seed sprouted each morning. She began to talk to her plants. Sometimes, she'd ask them what they needed. Other times, she would thank them for being pretty.

Mitch suffers from PTSD after having served two terms in the Vietnam War. Sometimes, his mind takes him places he doesn't want to visit. Having a way to keep his mind busy has helped his symptoms a great deal.

Getting his hands in the dirt calms him, too. There was only one problem. Mitch's back pain made it difficult for him to work in the garden. Bending to the ground was both painful and problematic. There were moments when he wasn't sure he'd be able to get back up.

Mitch asked their college instructor whether she had any ideas on gardening with back pain. The instructor recommended a few books and the *Self Sufficient Me* YouTube channel. Mitch wasn't much of a reader, but Lucy was. She dove right into the task.

Neither Mitch nor Lucy had ever used YouTube. They thought it was a mess of funny cat videos. It was surprising to them that they could actually find useful information there. Mitch started searching YouTube using phrases like "gardening for retirees." He also searched "gardening with back problems" and "gardening for cheap." He found a few channels that gave him numerous ideas.

It looked like a raised bed garden was a good option for reducing back pain from bending. Because they were living on a slender budget, they needed to build one from reused material. They visited their local grocery store to see whether there were any wood pallets that were being thrown away. With seven wood pallets in Mitch's small pickup truck, they were ready to build a raised bed.

Mitch wasn't a carpenter, but he wasn't afraid to work with his hands. Lucy found a book that gave them step-by-step instructions on how to build a raised bed from pallets. It would have taken them a lot of energy to do it themselves.

They came up with a plan to get some help and have fun doing it. Instead of a barn-raising party, they hosted a bed-raising party.

Lucy made a giant stack of hamburgers. Her two grown children, plus their grandkids, came with work pants on and hammers in hand. Their neighbor wanted to learn how to make a raised bed, and she came offering nails and screws. One of their cousins had just trimmed the bushes in front of his house. He brought a load of twigs and leaves to fill the bottom of the raised bed.

Within two hours, the raised bed was finished. Mitch used an old lawn chair to test out whether he could sit and reach the top of the bed. He was then able to snip off leaves of kale with ease. Their crowd of loved ones cheered as Mitch raised his hands in the air and yelled, "Score!"

Asking for help has always been difficult for Mitch. But that day, he saw things differently. He noticed the huge smile on Lucy's face as she watched their youngest granddaughter plant the first seed. Their neighbor thanked him for showing her that she could garden, too. The family decided that the following month, they would do it again, only at the neighbor's house.

By asking for help, Mitch created space for his community to expand. He often felt like family BBQs were nice but boring. He relished getting things done. This bed-raising gave him the best of both worlds—a connection to his community and a job well done.

After that first bed-raising, things began to change in Lucy and Mitch's world. Their once isolated existence consisted of listing off ailments whenever their kids called. Once they started gardening, they couldn't wait to talk about the happenings. What's in season? What's struggling to grow? Lucy's daughter noticed a lightness in her mom's voice during their visits.

They began hosting monthly garden gatherings. Their grandchildren and their friends would come and work in the garden. Their yard was bustling with visitors. Folks wanted fresh produce from the tiny stand they had on their front lawn. Many retirees came by to learn how to garden.

Six months into gardening, Mitch and Lucy started offering retiree gardening classes. These events always included lunch and conversation. The students came solely via word of mouth, as Lucy and Mitch were not interested in marketing.

Mitch embraces his new hobby. He has the satisfaction he received from years of full-time work without the stress. When his PTSD kicks up, he goes out into the garden to see what needs to be done. After fifteen minutes of pruning or planting, he feels calmer. He calls it dirt therapy.

Lucy is naturally a social butterfly. Having people over for tea is a huge benefit of learning to garden. She delights in spending quality time with her grandkids. It is a treat to meet their young friends and watch their interactions.

After a day of visitors, her heart is full each evening. She sits in her recliner and opens whatever book she is currently reading. Her sleep is deep and restful.

By default, both Mitch and Lucy are eating more fruits and vegetables. It is the easiest fast food they have available. Instead of a thirty-minute trek to the grocery store, they walk out into their garden. They pick a green bell pepper, tomatoes, and chard for a delicious omelet.

With their curiosity awakened, everything is a new adventure.

Eggs? Could they raise hens? Didn't they have a neighbor who raised hens? Maybe they could barter fresh garden veggies for eggs. And they did just that. More connections ensued.

Every Monday, they visit Leila and swap veggies for eggs. They spend a few minutes chatting about how her newest chicken is getting along with the others. Or how the recent cold spell surprised their basil. Yet another deepening of friendship is occurring.

They make a nice chunk of change from their small stand in the front yard. It provides wealth that they reinvest in their garden. They took some of their earnings and enrolled in a compost workshop.

It bothered Mitch to throw their pruning waste into the garbage. He learned that those bits could be made into nutritious compost. He and Lucy were interested in saving money on fertilizer and soil. Composting would help cut expenses.

Next stop? Compost class for Mitch!

The compost class seemed a bit complicated. There were thermostats and formulas. Mitch intuitively felt like there must be an easier way. Food left on the forest floor rots fine without someone taking its temperature.

He mentioned this in passing to the clerk at his regular garden center. The salesclerk recommended David The Good's book *Compost Everything*. Mitch has trouble reading books, but he enjoys the audiobook that his daughter bought him. The audio version of this book was not available, but Lucy was happy to read him a page each night. It made for interesting evening discussions.

Mitch also dove right into David The Good's YouTube channel. This gardener is exactly his style. No formulas—a little bit of humor—easy-to-understand instructions.

They started a compost pile based on David's ideas. It's tucked behind the garage. Once a week, Lucy takes a freezer bag of kitchen scraps out of the freezer and dumps it on a pile of crushed leaves. She makes what another YouTuber, Anne of All Trades, describes as compost apartments.

The green material (veggie cuttings, old flowers, fruit cores) is nestled into a pile of brown material (crushed dry leaves, dry grass clippings, shredded paper) and covered with more brown material to create the roof of the apartment.

Lucy and Mitch are very mellow with their compost making. After they created a three-foot-high compost pile, they considered turning it. And I do mean "considered." It is their least favorite job on hot days, and it can be hard labor if they try to do it quickly. So, they consider it.

Is today a good day? Too hot? Never mind. Is their grandson coming over tomorrow? Maybe he can do it. Let's wait. They never, ever turn it as much as the compost class instructed, but they are in no rush.

One day, they noticed it. The sign from the earth that every compost composer wants to see. They had grubs in their pile. And those grubs went to work. The compost started to look like the compost in all those YouTube videos they watched. Next, earthworms found their pile. Lucy couldn't wait to call her daughter and tell her about the worm party happening in their backyard.

Composting was marvelous for their garden. The plants loved it. They were able to mix it with dirt from their yard and lower the cost of soil needed from the garden store. It is marvelous for Lucy as well.

She became fascinated by the transmutation of waste to garden gold. This is a hilarious turn of events as Lucy was not initially a fan of composting. More on that later.

All of that has changed! Turning the compost pile gives her a satisfaction like no other. For years, she worried about all the trash her family created. Vegetable scraps thrown in a plastic trash bag and piled up in a landfill made her sad. Before composting, she felt helpless. She worked fifty hours a week and raised two kids with very little time to consider making any changes.

With a few small changes, Lucy was able to cut her weekly waste by the bagful. She's also taught her children and grandchildren how to do it. Their newfound knowledge is influencing generations. This thought gives her immense peace when her head hits the pillow each evening.

Her children both have low-maintenance compost piles in their yards. They called their mom a few times for reassurance that they were doing it right, and now it's old hat. They no longer throw compostable paper like egg cartons in the trash. Instead, they walk them out to the compost bin. Viola! Garden gold is made.

Lucy wanted to create even more compost gold. She and Mitch put their heads together. Every Thursday, they drive to town for errands and have breakfast at the local diner. What if they composted the diner's coffee grounds?

The diner was more than happy to save a few bags of coffee grounds for them. Mitch gave the owner two five-gallon buckets to fill up each week. They brought the grounds home to make new compost apartments on their pile. They swap out empty buckets for full buckets every week.

They started selling buckets of compost at their farm stand as well. They also invite their neighbor's chickens over once a month to scratch through the compost. It is a win-win compost agreement.

The chickens scratch through the pile. This turns the pile and adds bits of nutrient-dense chicken manure to the compost. The birds are well fed with a protein-rich feast of grubs and other insects in the pile.

Mitch and Lucy have created a life as rich as their homegrown compost. In part two, we'll look at how they did this. And that will translate to how *you* can do it, too.

EASY-BREEZY END OF CHAPTER TASKS

- Mitch found a few ways to work around his back pain. What types of ailments are keeping you from doing something you'd like? Write a quick list in your Homesteader Mindset Journal.

- Are there ways that you can work around your ailments? Brainstorm three activities that will enrich your life without harming your body.

- Mitch has trouble reading. So, he found other ways to learn about things that were important to him. Do you have trouble with a certain type of learning? Are there other options for you? Write a few down. If you can't think of alternatives, consider searching online for topics like *how to learn when you don't like to [read]*.

PART TWO

THREE POWERFUL ACTIONS TO MASTER

A number of things may have happened to you while reading part one of this book. Perhaps you felt excited at the possibility of change in your life, and you can't wait to get started.

Maybe you found yourself shaking your head. You thought to yourself, *Look at this mountain of change I need to make! A homesteader mindset seems farther away than ever.*

The purpose of part one was to show you what's available. There are countless ways you can create a homesteader mindset. But how? How do we get from where we are at this very minute? How do we find ourselves with our feet in the grass, smiling up at the sun (with closed eyes, please)?

Part two is going to take you deep into the *how* of a homesteader mindset. We'll be walking through three actions that will lead to mindset shifts. Once the mind turns its gears in the direction of a solution, miracles occur.

Being the very practical person that I am, I start with actions that will shift my mind. You can absolutely do it the other way around, too. Thoughts can create actions that will shift the mind. As a matter of fact, reading this book is one way that you are gathering new thoughts to create change.

Does all this talk about action tire you out? Are you resistant to grabbing a scrub brush? Does putting some elbow grease into your life circumstances seem unappealing? Well, you're in luck. The three actions that we will be discussing, *play*, *learn*, and *do now*, are actually more fun than work.

That's the secret to creating a homesteader mindset. It's about enjoyment, energy building, and, dare I say it, adventure. Who doesn't want a little more discovery and wonder in their life? Let's take the plunge and explore together.

CHAPTER 4

WHAT'S PLAY GOT TO DO WITH IT?

Oh. Oh. Oh. What's play got to do? Got to do with it? Yes, Tina Turner's song is running through my mind as I type this.

Play helps the brain connect new neural pathways. If you see play and creation as a dual action, you will be on the lookout for ways to make tasks fun.

Some folks are curious by nature. Curiosity is also a talent you can develop. If you find yourself chatting with someone, ask about how they got where they are today. You will either learn how to get on a similar path to what they have achieved or you will know what not to do if they are going in the opposite direction of your vision.

From questions, you can learn wonderful tidbits about life. What prompted that millionaire contractor to start a business? How did the expat songwriter decide to up and move to Portugal?

And bonus! You will also become a more interesting person. Bored people are so freaking, well, boring. Don't be boring. Be curious. Learn to ask questions.

Your curiosity muscle will build the more you look for aspects of life that interest you. Curiosity is an important part of my job as an acupuncturist. I need to find the pattern that is causing the reason for my patient's visit to the clinic. I am receptive to every ounce of information the patient shares with me. The way they walk can tell me where their pain might be. The odor on their breath can tell me something is out of balance. And, of course, what they tell me about their health concerns gives me additional clues.

The same is true about daily encounters outside of the clinic. People tell me all sorts of neat things. I merely take what works and leave the rest.

One of the themes I've gathered from my informal, everyday research is this. Successful people give themselves permission to play. Some won't call it that. They might use the word create instead. Others will tell you, "I work hard at something I love." Working on a passion project is a form of play.

Let's go back to those earlier questions.

The contractor? He helped his friend restore a run-down Victorian on the weekends. He found immense pleasure in creating a home with a traditional vibe. That was the niche company he built.

He built the company on the weekends while working reduced hours at his day job. He looked forward to his weekends. His wife would pop over to the project and bring lunch. They'd sit outside and talk about what their new business would look like. The building of his business was fun. It infused him and his family with hope.

We can learn a great deal from the contractor. Doing things that come naturally to you is a clue that it might be a solid path. Before writing a book, I wrote all the time.

I've been journaling since I was fifteen or so. Writing comes easily to me. I gave my writing away to self-help organizations. I landed a gig as a content developer for a language-learning blog. Those seemingly unconnected stepping stones—journaling, volunteering, blogging—got me to where I am right now. Writing a book is full-on playtime for me!

The songwriter expat who moved to Portugal? He visited the country for a family wedding. For the bachelor party, the wedding party visited a piano bar. He offered to perform a few songs while the piano player was on his break, and his songs brought down the house. When the owner offered him a weekend gig, he declined. Once back in the States, he kept asking himself, *Why not?*

He played with the numbers. On lunch breaks, he would scribble down what kind of cash it would take to move. He would imagine himself in Portugal. These ideas gave him energy.

He purchased a travel magazine that featured Portugal. He'd spend hours pouring over articles of places he'd like to visit. Each minute that he spent daydreaming and planning brought him one step closer to his goal.

Let's look at how Lucy used play to establish her homesteader mindset. She developed a habit of play and creation before retirement. Only she didn't consciously realize the habit. Lucy simply enjoyed certain routines and rituals.

Her early morning reading afforded her a break from the everyday grind before her family woke up. She had carved out this time early in her marriage. Even when her children were little, they knew to leave mom alone until after 6 a.m.

The wee hours of the morning were her time. She was a voracious reader of mystery novels. And the novels offered her a respite. She enjoyed the scenes of faraway places that the authors described. Because of this habit, her vocabulary was impressive.

Her ability to articulate her thoughts helped her in her professional life. She had a job that was mentally tasking. At times, the work required intense focus. But she made room for quiet contemplation during her work week.

Her lunch hour was sacred. As soon as she finished her to-do list, she would put her phone on silent, grab her bagged lunch, and head to the park. It took her fifteen minutes to pack up and drive to the park and fifteen minutes to get back to work. She savored the thirty minutes of peace she would feel as she sat on a park bench and enjoyed her meal.

Sometimes, she would watch children playing in the distance. Other times, she would enjoy the quiet that the trees provided. This hour away from it all gave her the mental rest she needed to return to work, energized.

On Saturdays, she would spend time with her daughter's children. She took them to the park for playtime. Or she'd have a movie day at her house.

Movie days always involved a long neighborhood walk to stretch her legs. It helped release some of their youthful energy, too.

After the grandchildren went to bed, a serious game of pinochle would ensue. Their best friends, Joanie and Gil, would often pop over for snacks and a card game. Sometimes her daughter and son-in-law would join in the fun. There was a lot of laughter and teasing during these games.

If you asked Lucy, she would say these moments were her sanity-keepers.

After retirement, she kept up her morning coffee and book ritual. But the park lunches disappeared. Her grandchildren were starting to enjoy their social circles more and more. Life got small.

When Mitch got revved up about creating a garden, Lucy caught some of his enthusiasm. She started finding ways to incorporate play into their gardening. Some of it was simply built around work. She'd ask her grandson to come over and help build a duck house. She suggested they celebrate the completion of each task for the duck house with a card game.

For example, they'd get supplies for the duck house. Then, they'd enjoy a card game before saying goodbye. It was a combo deal that suited her and her grandson well.

And so, her weeks began to fill with a little work and a lot of joy.

She set her sights on things that gave her pleasure and let the rest fall a bit to the side. So what if her kale needed pruning? She was okay with letting it go for a week because she was having fun learning to raise ducks. As it turns out, ducks like eating kale. The leaves that she eventually pruned gave her glee as she watched her ducks enjoy them for lunch.

For most of her life, she was responsible. She carried more than her share of worry and duty. With the garden, she let go of that heaviness. Because she was experimenting with permaculture, less daily organization needed to be done. Most of their routine involved maintenance of the food forest they'd developed.

What is permaculture?

It's an agricultural design system where the goal is self-regeneration. A gardener or farmer plants mostly perennials in groups called guilds. These plants have a number of functions to help each other, help wildlife, and feed their humans.

I will be discussing permaculture in a follow-up book as a part of my *The Homesteader Mindset* series. This is one of my favorite discoveries. And I cannot wait to share it with you.

Before we continue, I would like to explain the concept of a food forest. That's what many permaculturists call their gardens. They model their plot after an actual forest. This can be done on a large scale or in someone's tiny backyard. It can also be created in any growing zone.

Do you have four seasons? It'll work. Live in the desert? It'll work. Swamp? Well, your plant selection will change and you'll need some hip boots. But yes, it'll still work.

Can you tell that I'm excited about permaculture? Oh, my goodness!

Let's get back to Lucy's story.

She was as excited as I was about permaculture. With it, she is able to create a park-like setting in her backyard. No more lawn that sucks up way too much water and doesn't offer food for her family or shelter for wildlife. And best of all, she has a tranquil place to relax in the afternoon, much like her lunch break excursions.

This project gives her such bliss. She sometimes has a hard time containing herself. She switched her morning reading to books about permaculture. Memoirs are her favorite, but the how-to books offer a ton of innovative ideas.

She keeps a journal near her books for jotting down ideas she likes. She also makes a to-do list on the first empty page of each book with new books to read and tasks she'd like to try.

Learning the language of permaculture makes her feel vibrant and alive. She can't wait to sit down with her books in the morning. When Mitch wakes up, she fills him in on her newest findings. Their breakfast conversation is filled with brainstorming and excitement.

And it all started with Lucy making space for play. If she doesn't like a particular task, she is completely okay with putting it off for a while as she does something fun. As it turns out, Mitch and Lucy have different ideas of fun.

Mitch has no interest in dealing with the compost pile. He appreciates the result but doesn't relish the idea of playing with worms, whereas Lucy revels in composting. She is absolutely amazed by the change from trash to treasure.

Mitch finds pruning to be especially satisfying. Perhaps it is his love of tidiness that motivates him. He feels like a kid in a candy store when comfortably sitting on his garden stool with pruners in hand. There is a unique thrill he experiences when he steps back and sees the instant result of his pruning. More sunlight hitting the plants. Cleaner plot. Happy looking garden.

Play comes in different packages for Mitch and Lucy. They allow themselves the time to figure out what endeavors gave them joy. Working with different preferences is key.

You might be thinking to yourself, "Well, this is all fine and good for Mitch and Lucy, but what about me? How in the world am I going to make space for play in my life when I barely have time for sleep?" I'll be answering that in part four of this book. Right now, we're laying down the foundation. The windows with a view will be installed with the Pocket Puzzle Plan.

Please take a moment to reflect and write your answers to the following questions.

EASY-BREEZY END OF CHAPTER TASKS

- Think of a routine (current or long ago) that gave you tremendous joy. Write down what you loved about it. Use all five senses.

- Take the things that you enjoyed in item one and write three ways you could get that type of joy in your life right now.

- What do the words "play" and "create" evoke in you? What are the messages you've learned about those words? How can you increase the positive aspects and decrease the stumbling blocks?

CHAPTER 5

BUILD YOUR FOUNDATION BY LEARNING

Let's build your foundation with the powerful action of learning. In this chapter, we'll talk about the why. In the following chapter, we'll delve into the how of this important discipline.

I know you're more than capable of learning because you've gotten this far into the book. No matter what madness sits outside the space between you and this page, you are here. You are learning. You are looking for options. For that, I'd like to take a moment and give you a round of applause.

I'm not kidding. You're past the introductory stories. You've got your Homesteader Mindset Journal, I hope. If not, please get a few scraps of paper and review the previous chapter questions.

You are soaking up new ideas and deciding what might work for you and what you can put aside for now. That is a feat. To make your applause special, I'm going to give it to you in three languages. The following information is quite accurate, according to a very scientific cartoon meme.

I found it moments before typing this sentence. Yes, I am that dedicated to true research.

English:	Clap. Clap. Clap.
Indonesian:	Prok. Prok. Prok.
Arabic:	Stah. Stah. Stah.

Why the three versions of applause? I am a language nerd. I learned how to speak French and Spanish in my forties after failing at language learning ten times. Hey, everyone knows eleven's a charm!

What was the secret I found the eleventh time? I didn't give up after my tenth failure.

I stumbled upon a polyglot, Benny Lewis, who explained how to learn a language by speaking from day one. A polyglot is someone who speaks multiple languages. Benny speaks ten or more different languages. If you're interested in learning a language, visit his website. It's Fluentin3months.com.

I was such a huge fan of Fluent in 3 Months that they eventually hired me to develop content and coach their students. It is an amazing job. And it isn't just because I work with a lot of creative, interesting people; I get paid to learn.

My mentor at Fi3M, David Masters, taught me how to write for a blog. I learned how to make YouTube videos and edit podcast recordings. The biggest benefit is that I learn directly from the polyglots I interview.

Language learning is a passion project of mine. Learning is fun. It feels like play because I use techniques that motivate me. My learning style fits my personality and routine.

Of course, everything about learning isn't fun. I'm not a huge fan of learning grammar (and it shows when I'm having a conversation in French at a party). With the tricky but important things I need to learn, I take them in minuscule bits. I mean itty-bitty, teeny-weeny morsels.

Language learning is a huge part of my homesteader mindset. It showed me a great deal about my strengths and weaknesses.

Why is learning such a big part of a homesteader mindset?

You feel more alive.

When you have something that stimulates your mind, you want to wake up in the morning. You can't wait to get out of bed and spend ten minutes on your project before your day starts. We'll talk more about how to find time and energy for your projects in part four of this book.

What moments have you wasted by scrolling through social media or nursing resentment? They are replaced with thoughts of what's coming around the corner in your learning journey. Instead of numbing out with TV, you'll be waking up your senses.

A homesteader mindset is all about being present in your day. Having a learning project like building pantry shelves will focus your attention. You will be more seated in the here and now.

One of my favorite passages in the *Big Book of Alcoholics Anonymous* is by a doctor who was in recovery. He wrote, "When I stopped living in the problem and began living in the answer, the problem went away." This is something I discuss with my patients who are suffering from addiction.

It's not just for alcoholics, either. I have had periods in my life where I was stuck in negative thinking. I focused on the problems, and the problems increased.

Have you ever seen the face or vase optical illusion? It's usually a black-and-white image. If you concentrate on the black section in the middle, you see a vase. If you focus on the white sections around the vase, you see a face on either side.

The brain is a marvelous organ. You might think that you can see both the faces and the vase at the same time. What's really happening is your brain is switching rapidly between both images. Face. Vase. Face. Vase. So fast that you think you're seeing them simultaneously.

Our brains can only focus on one main conscious idea at a time, which is understandable, don't you think? It has lots of tasks to do while focusing your conscious thinking. It's balancing you upright as you sit reading this book. It's moving your eyes from one word to the next. It's monitoring your temperature and will let you know if you need to put on a sweater. It's truly remarkable.

But it can only do so much. It can't see the problem and the solution at the same time.

Learning something new helps your brain. By having a goal of learning a new skill, you are actively creating a solution for your life. Maybe it's learning how to bake a quiche. If you're not getting enough protein in your diet, baking a quiche will provide you with three or more servings in a week. You can freeze some of it. As a bonus, it solves a budget problem as cooking at home is economical.

If the big-picture problem arises in your mind, gently remind yourself that you are in the process of solving it. "Yes, I need more protein in my diet. That is why I am learning how to bake a quiche. I will focus on that task."

This allows you to give yourself a break from the long lists of shoulds. Start with one. Give yourself permission to enjoy learning. Add another once the new skill is a habit.

But how do you have fun learning to cook when you hate it? We'll learn more about this from Jim and Sara's story later in this chapter. First, let's look at the second reason learning is a big part of a homesteader mindset.

Your brain grows and stays healthier longer.

Neuroscience is a fascinating topic. We know so little. Every year, there is a new discovery about the brain. For the longest time, scientists believed that the brain stops growing at a certain age. They theorized you grew new neurons as a child and young adult, and then you capped out during adulthood.

If you were a stubborn chump at age thirty, you were lost cause.

Recently, studies have shown that our brains keep creating new neurons. We create even more when we exercise regularly and learn new skills.

Lucky you! There are a ton of skills in homesteading that include exercise while learning. Pruning a bush or hanging laundry to dry are two examples. It's not extreme sweat like boot camp in the gym, but it is something your body benefits from doing. Movement.

In traditional Chinese medicine, moving the body to the point of excessive sweating is far from ideal. It wastes precious yin fluids, which can't be regenerated with a swig of blue energy drink. As an acupuncturist, I talk a lot about the loss of yin fluids in the clinic. Slow and steady movement is best.

As for learning, it does some really neat things. Learning a new skill will actually change the structure of your brain. It will reorganize thought patterns. This is exciting news!

If you've often been unlucky with your choices in life, learning a new skill can change those habit patterns. It can help you see things differently. Thereby making better decisions and ultimately changing your life.

From chump to champion, it's totally doable.

I became interested in how learning affects brain health while learning French. It was a wild experience the first few months of learning a language. I could feel new sensations in different parts of my brain. Perhaps it was because I had decades of body awareness meditation practice. Who knows!

It felt like I was waking up regions of my brain that I'd never used. Have you ever tried a new workout? Do you remember what it felt like the next day? You're surprised to feel soreness in muscles you never knew you had. The brain sensation wasn't discomfort. It felt like I was getting blood flow to new areas. It was wild.

Most people already know we only use a small fraction of our brain in daily life. Here's the surprising news. We gain access to more brain activity as we learn something new.

There is a study floating around that every polyglot seems to know. Learning a language can prevent or postpone dementia. People who speak more than one language have healthier brains. Signs of dementia occur ten or more years later than their monolingual counterparts. Imagine ten more years of a healthy brain simply because you learned something new.

Let's just name it. Language skills and brain health go together like baked pear and Christmas.

On a side note, you can add "baked pear" to your learn list. It's super simple, amazingly delicious, and refined sugar-free. It's so easy, in fact, that I've added a link to the recipe at the end of this book. I cannot let you put this book down without the immediate win of making winterlicious baked pear. Send me a pic of your first batch!

Back to learning and slowing dementia: I'm convinced that learning any new skill will help you with brain health. If you exercise one part of your brain, you're bringing oxygenated blood to other parts of the brain at the same time.

You attract more cool people into your life because you are cooler.

This is where the going gets good. As you begin to find subjects that fascinate you, you'll be more interesting to others. And vice versa, your newly found love of learning will make you curious about others.

No, this is not my "How to Win Friends and Influence People" section of the book. However, I am going to talk a bit about community. We humans are social creatures.

Yes, even introverts are social animals. Look at the "how dare you call and not text" memes and witty "leave me alone" T-shirts. People are confusing introversion with disconnection.

There's a lot of hype around being a lone wolf. It's hip to want to be alone with your cell phone apps day in and day out. Only that's not a lone wolf. That's a by-product of marketing that conned you into believing you don't need anything but products to be happy.

If you must be a lone wolf, do it right. A lone wolf walks outside in nature a lot. Start there. Ditch your phone for hours or days at a time. I do. It's fun.

Introverts need a good amount of alone time to fill their energy cup. You can be an introvert and have a homesteader mindset. One that appreciates community and family. It's important to find ways to connect that work for you and your psychological preferences. We'll dive deeper into introversion and extroversion in just a minute.

First, let me explain the cool factor. How on earth does learning help you attract cool people into your life? Well, let's start with what exactly "cool" means in this claim.

Cool is something a person finds attractive or impressive.

What's cool to me may or may not be cool to you.

Yesterday, I met a patient who was trilingual. He spoke English, German, and Spanish. I know this because he had a slight accent. I used two sentences I remember in German: "Do you speak German? I speak English, Spanish, and French."

We then had a conversation in Spanish. We talked about how he learned those three languages. I got a fascinating glimpse into his life. He was the coolest person I'd met all day. Why? Because his language skills impressed me. And because I'm a language learner.

If I had no interest in languages, I probably wouldn't have even asked what languages he speaks. But because I'm keen to practice my target languages as much as possible, I always ask. It turns out, people love talking about language learning, especially when they've learned several. I attract cool people because I have the intriguing hobby of learning languages.

What about introverted people? They could never do that, right? Wrong, my friend. I'm one of the most introverted people I know. Language learning comes easily to me because I foster an appropriate framework.

We'll talk about personality tendencies and learning styles in the next chapter. It's one of my favorite topics, as it can change the way you approach new experiences.

EASY-BREEZY END OF CHAPTER TASKS

- Think of a time when you felt truly alive and awake. Even if it's something you can't do right now, think about how it made you feel. Maybe it was the feeling of freedom during an impromptu dance party in your pjs. Explore the memory. What did it feel like in your body?

- Dissect the moment further. In what way could you recreate that feeling? Is there some way to learn more about that experience? Perhaps an online class? Maybe a community event?

- Who in your life do you think is cool? What is it that attracts you to them? Is it possible that something they have is something you want? I've always been drawn to my friends who are authors. No surprise that I'm an author now. Perhaps your friend's cool attribute is something you would like to acquire. Write it down in your Homesteader Mindset Journal.

CHAPTER 6

HOW TO BEST LEARN FOR YOUR PERSONALITY

INTROVERSION AND EXTROVERSION

Most introverted people prefer a less stimulating environment. Especially highly sensitive people. Extroverted people prefer more stimulating environments. These are keys to your learning style.

An extrovert might find a conference the best motivation for learning new skills. There are numerous classes to attend—tons of new people to meet—lots of interesting conversations happening. If this is you, consider booking a trip to a nearby homesteading conference. You can learn more from the speakers that are listed on the schedule by checking out their websites, too.

An introvert might find reading numerous books on the subject more accessible. That doesn't mean an introvert should never meet other homesteaders. He might want to do it in smaller doses. Small gatherings and bookstores are great places for an introverted person to start. Inviting another homesteader to tea is a low-stimulation option.

Let's look at Sara and Jim to see how they manage it.

Sara and Jim are opposites when it comes to psychological preference. Jim charges his emotional battery with social interaction. He enjoys dinner parties, meeting new people, and group adventures. If he had to spend a week alone in the house, he would be bouncing off the walls.

Sara needs time alone to recharge. She prefers quiet hours over energetic social interaction. She loves having one-on-one conversations, walking in nature, and reading books. She enjoys a routine that includes planned solitude.

One of Jim's favorite ways to learn is verbally. We'll talk more about learning styles later, as it's another set of keys to unlocking the powerful tool of learning. Since Jim thrives on learning through conversation, a large event is a great place for him.

Through conversation, he assembles new ideas. Collaborating with others gives him energy and purpose. He thinks out loud and processes his concepts by working through them with others.

He spends more time in the hallway chatting with other attendees than in the classrooms. That's where he discusses his ideas and gets tips on how he can improve. He makes friends with people who share his interests. He often invites them over for dinner to continue the friendship.

Sara processes her thoughts differently than Jim. She journals every morning for ten minutes. She writes about her past, present, and future.

In her journal, she writes about significant events that happened. It's her way of sorting through her emotions. This journal is private. So, she's okay with misspelled words and incoherent sentences. She uses it to empty her mind before starting the day.

At times, she makes a gratitude list. In it, she lists everything she can think of that is good in her life. It can be as simple as a warm bed. Or as heartfelt as her son's empathy for another boy. Or as vast as her appreciation for regenerative agriculture.

She writes about projects. She lists what she needs to do that day in the garden. She scribbles down a few questions she needs to have answered about how to harvest and save seeds. These questions will get transferred to her day planner as tasks for later in the week.

Much of her mental process occurs in silence. She doesn't have the same desire as Jim to brainstorm with others. She will usually save that for when a project is in the works. She's open to new ideas on how to improve things, and she welcomes conversations about it from people on her team. Usually, those conversations happen one-on-one and at scheduled times.

Because Jim and Sara savor their connection to each other as well, they find ways to bring their two worlds together. Every morning over breakfast, they talk about happenings in their lives. The boys talk about their news. Jim and Sara chat about their projects.

Sara listens and asks questions when others discuss their ideas. Jim enjoys throwing a new idea on the table and hearing what everyone thinks about it. Their sons like being a part of the creation process and oftentimes come up with great insight. Jim and Sara love laughing with their boys. Making daily contact with them around the breakfast table is as nutritious as the meal.

The breakfast chat is usually energetic and fun. This fills up Jim's cup. The boys feel heard. Sara joins in the conversation fully. She talks about her projects, too.

Yet, Sara needs a different type of connection. She and Jim take long walks together to give her quiet space to share her thoughts with him. The boys often come along but are busy discovering new lands as they climb hills and jump over streams.

Sara finds ways to connect with each of her sons in a quiet manner, too. One of her boys loves to do puzzles. So, Sara brings her crochet project and sits with him while he plays. She has a similar quiet time with her other son, who is fond of building things. They are constructing a patio bench together.

In this way, both Sara and Jim get their needs met. Once Sara realized that she was introverted, she started to nurture her solitude. She limits her social gatherings to events that are important to her. She made a few rules to keep her from falling into the trap of doing too much. Her body thanked her for it with increased energy and focus.

This doesn't mean that Jim is the only person to make new friends. Sure, he often brings home interesting people to join their community. Sara happily converses with everyone for the first hour or so.

Then she does something remarkable. She excuses herself from the gathering and goes into a quiet area of the house to read.

I know! My jaw dropped, too, when I heard this. How is that even allowed?! The beautiful thing is that it has become routine. Her friends expect to see her for about an hour or so. She and Jim drive separate cars so that she can leave when her social cup is full.

I am such a fan of this idea. It's my new normal. Last night, we went to a large neighborhood gathering. I couldn't wait to attend because I knew that I could leave whenever I wanted. About ninety minutes into the event, I slipped out of the house. A few neighbors asked me where I was going. I explained, "I had a wonderful time, but this introvert needs to go home and read a book." That was it. It was so easy. If only I had known this years ago!

My husband, the social butterfly of our family, stayed another four hours. Four hours! If I had stayed, there would have been nothing left of me but a shrunken head. Yet, his extroverted cup was filled to the brim. He loved it.

Okay. Enough of my personal introvert wins. What about Sara?

Does she only meet friends through Jim? No. Sara finds other ways to engage and share learning experiences.

If she sees a neighbor working in their front yard while she's walking her dog, she'll compliment their garden. The neighbor will usually respond with a comment about this or that plant. The next thing you know, Sara has learned three new gardening techniques in the span of six minutes.

No preparation needed. Low stimulation environment. After a few of these conversations, Sara may invite the neighbor over to see her garden. The next thing you know, they are swapping cuttings.

Some introverts might think, "But what if I don't have time to talk the next day? I'll never be able to walk that street again." It's all about setting appropriate boundaries and using clear body language.

On days when Sara needs to get going on her walk, she greets the neighbor while continuing to move forward. If the neighbor asks her a question, she'll answer and continue walking. If the neighbor doesn't notice and keeps talking, she'll kindly say, "I'd love to chat with you today, but I'm on a tight schedule. Maybe later this week, I'll have more time." And off she goes.

In this way, she allows herself room to take care of herself. She doesn't worry too much about what others might think of her. Easier said than done? It's easier done than said.

Overthinking gets people in trouble with setting boundaries. Practice helps.

When Sara first started practicing boundaries like this, it was hard to contemplate. She told herself that she was going to experiment with body language. It could be a means of setting appropriate boundaries. The first time she did it, she got so flustered that she walked straight into a bush.

The next morning at breakfast, she recounted the story with her family. Her storytelling talent and their laughter took the sting out of her awkwardness. The second time she set a boundary, it was easier. The fifth time felt nearly graceful. Now, it's a walk in the park rather than a walk into a bush.

The secret here is that Jim and Sara figured out what suits their individual personalities. For Sara, that meant reading books on introversion and highly sensitive people. For Jim, that meant being aware of what types of interactions fill him up. What are some of your favorite activities for filling up your energy cup?

It doesn't have to fit an introversion/extroversion profile, as we all have bits of each in our preferences. For example, Sara's social side comes out with exercise. Taking a weekly dance class and chatting it up with classmates is a great way for her to connect. None of her classmates even know she's an introvert.

FOUR LEARNING STYLES

There are numerous learning styles. I've narrowed the list to the four most common. Let's look at how they are used when learning a homesteader mindset skill. I use these four learning styles as a starting point for language learners I coach.

One of my past students is an educator. She pitched a fit when I mentioned these. To save my readers' elevated blood pressure, I would like to address some of the issues she brought up.

- No one person fits into just one learning style. We do well with a mix of them.
- Learning styles are techniques for acquiring information. They are not categories of people.
- She thinks this system is outdated. I like it for helping students choose habits for their learning toolbox.

Whew. Now that my lovely readers are within a healthy blood pressure range, let's continue.

The visual, audio, read/write, and kinesthetic (VARK) model was developed in 1992 by Neil Fleming and Colleen Mills. They wanted to explain how best to share and receive information when teaching.

Visual style is also sometimes called graphic, which would make the acronym much more fun, GARK. It sounds like something a purple-striped alien puppet would utter. "GARK!"

Visual style refers to learning through drawings, maps, graphs, and the like.

Jim uses drawings when he is building something. He needs to see a version of it on paper to work out what needs to go where. When he is learning a new skill, he draws as someone describes the project to him. In one case, it was learning how to create a water-retaining swale.

To understand the dynamics of a swale, Jim studies the drawing. A napkin or a scrap of paper will suffice. He uses his doodle to verify that he understands the concept. This is an example of visual learning.

If you're curious about swales, check out your online book bonus guide. Visit: www.createwellnessproject.com/bookbonus. I list several articles and videos on swales. Geoff Lawton is the swale master. You'll learn a great deal from him. His links are available in the Permaculture section.

I will mention this book bonus throughout the book so that you don't have to search for it when you are ready to use it. I also put it at the front of the book for you.

Audio style is fairly easy to explain. Many of us do it on a daily basis. It's learning through listening.

Sara does this every day in several ways. She listens to a podcast on homesteading while hanging laundry on the clothesline. On her commute to work, she enjoys an audiobook she borrowed from the library using the Libby app. Her audiobooks are usually memoirs of a minimalist or gardener. They offer her light education and heavy inspiration on her drive.

Don't fret. I've got you covered! I compiled a list of my favorite homesteading podcasts for you in the book bonus guide as well.

Listening isn't the most efficient way for Sara to learn. She doesn't consider audio her learning preference, but it works well with her schedule. Her mind wanders when she's listening to something. The information isn't retained as much as when she's reading and highlighting.

Audio learning is a compromise for Sara. She can utilize the time that would otherwise be spent without input. Sara gives herself permission to listen lightly. If her mind wanders, she gently brings it back to the audiobook or podcast. With light listening, it's okay to keep going rather than rewind and make sure you hear everything.

She is also careful not to fill every waking moment with audio learning. She gives herself lots of quiet time throughout the day as well. When she's in the garden, she prefers to keep her environment tranquil so that she can be more present.

Read/write style is a learning preference that involves absorbing information through reading books and writing.

This is Sara's favorite way to learn. She is a total bookworm. When she wants to learn more about a topic, it's not uncommon for her to read ten or more books on the subject.

To save money, she borrows books from the library. She periodically splurges on books so she can retain more by writing in the margins. That's the "write" part of this learning preference. Sometimes, she's merely writing out a piece of information in the margin exactly as it's written. This helps her remember the item better.

Sara is also big on writing lists. It's how she organizes her days and her projects. She feels better when she gets things out of her head onto paper.

As she is reading a book, she will create a to-do list based on the knowledge shared in the work.

Kinesthetic style is learning through doing.

This is where you have an idea about what you want to do, and you jump in and try it. YouTube tutorials are a free way to try your hand at kinesthetic learning.

Jim did it, too. He heard an interview with a man who used comfrey to create a border between his grass and his walking path. He had a walking path between his lawn and his garden that needed a border, but he wasn't interested in using stone. The next day, Jim broke up the roots from one of his sterile comfrey plants and planted them along the walking path. He learned by doing.

What about the fun factor that I mentioned earlier?

Jim and Sara use their learning preferences to make cooking a pleasant adventure. Jim is an extroverted master of doing. He enrolled in a cooking class while they were on vacation.

Jim learned how to make an Italian one-pot chicken and pasta dish. That was his jumping-off point. He uses YouTube videos to explore every dish his foodie heart desires. He is usually the cook when they host a dinner party at their home.

Sara motivates herself to learn how to cook by reading books about social change. *Radical Homemaker* by Shannon Hayes is one of her favorites. The more she learns about the slow food movement, the more she wants to rebel against the work-hard-eat-crap lifestyle.

She decided to learn batch cooking. In batch cooking, you make double the amount that you will eat for dinner. Then you freeze the extra servings for quick meal preps on busy nights.

Batch cooking works great in their household. Jim loves taking a glass container of beef stew to the office for lunch. All he needs to do is take it out of the freezer the night before work.

A casual Sunday evening finds the family in the kitchen. Jim is cooking a homemade meal. Sara is sitting at the kitchen table, pickling onions and garlic. Their boys are chopping up ginger for their favorite honey-fermented ginger treat. Sara glances at the garden bouquet she clipped moments before. She marvels at the beauty of blue basil flowers, lacy yarrow, and her family's chatter.

We haven't talked much about pickling via lacto-fermentation or honey-fermentation. It'll be discussed later in this book. We need to let the ideas ferment for a time. See what I did there?

EASY-BREEZY END OF CHAPTER TASKS

- What are the big-picture issues that are causing you worry? I'll list a few to help you get started.
  - Cost of living?
  - Sick family member?
  - Struggling with depression, anxiety, PTSD, or a combination of those?
  - Lonely?
  - Not enough quality time with family? Friends? Yourself?

- Choose two from the list and write down five things you could do to be in the solution. Make them easy actions to start. You don't need to know what to do with that list just yet. You're simply making space for a solution. Here are two examples.
  - You're worried about making ends meet. Write down "learn to cook rice" as one of your solutions.
  - Your loved one is ill and lives too far away to visit. Write down "send Aunt Sue a get-well letter."

- Dedicate a few pages in your Homesteader Mindset Journal for problem-to-solution pages. Fold the pages in half to make a crease down the middle of the page. At the top of the page, write "problem" on the left and "solution" on the right.
  - Whenever a problem pops up in your head, write it down. Then skip four lines before writing down the next problem. That will give you space for solutions on the other side of the crease.
  - Write down at least one solution for each issue before ending the session. You'll notice that throughout the day, solutions will pop into your mind. It doesn't matter how off the wall they are. Write them down on the solutions side.

CHAPTER 7

DO IT NOW

MAGIC MONDAYS DON'T EXIST

I'll start the garden on Monday.
One of these days,
I will eat dinner at the table instead of in front of the TV.
I'll get around to exercise when things settle down at work.

I've got news for you. Magical Monday never comes. If it does, it rarely sticks. It sets up a vicious cycle of screwing up on Tuesday and blowing the rest of the week until the next magical Monday arrives.

Dream big. Start small. But most of all, start.

~ Simon Sinek

The art of doing it now can change your life. This is not hyperbole. When you begin doing it now, you won't recognize your life in six months. It will have improved drastically.

"Do It Now" doesn't mean "Do it *all* right this minute." It's not about selling your entire stamp collection and placing a bet on red. Doing it now means you get started on that one thousand-mile journey with one little baby step.

What does starting small look like? Tamara is a perfect example.

In chapter two, Tamara changed her life from homesick-a-go-go to vibrant farm-in-the-city. Her extraordinary change started small and without much vision. She started with what she had.

In her case, it was the ability to read and a library card. Maybe your library is not a big deal to you, but it was to Tamara. The only library she had ever visited was her school library during study hall. She never once cracked open a book there. It was merely a room to pass the time between classes.

There is a public library two towns over from where Tamara grew up, but you can't get there unless you have a car. It's different now as you can use the online app, Libby, to borrow e-books on your phone. At the time, Tamara didn't know the Libby app existed.

Her very first action was to walk into the library after work. Her second important action was to ask the librarian whether there were any books on happiness. It took her fifteen minutes total to sign up for a library card and check out five books. That action created a positive snowball effect in her life.

Maybe you're not a reader, which is 100 percent fine. As explained in chapter six, we all have different learning preferences. Just for a minute, imagine you are a full-on library rat. What would be the subject that would inspire you to borrow a stack of books? Write that theme or themes in your Homesteader Mindset Journal now.

Nerdy language fact. Rat de bibliothèque (library rat) is French slang for the English term bookworm. Only it's a rodent. Why can't avid readers be referred to as something more appealing, like library tiger or book bear?

Do you want to know who you are? Don't ask. Act!
Action will delineate and define you.

~ Witold Gombrowicz

Tamara had no idea what she wanted to do with her life. The only thing she knew for certain was that she wanted to be happier. One of her library books shared a study: people with hobbies that use their hands are happier. She started asking her joyful customers whether they had a hobby. It was her informal poll.

Some of the hobbies seemed cool but were out of her reach financially. Some of them were downright awful in her mind. While considering what resonated with her, Tamara was learning more about herself. She didn't mind getting dirty, but she hated hobbies with tiny details.

She decided that walking daily would be her first hobby. It offered exercise. It piqued her curious nature to find new neighborhoods. It was how she stumbled upon the farmers' market. Walking fit her budget. The movement improved her mood.

If she feels a little down in the dumps, she notices that a thirty-minute walk gives her an immediate lift. About fifteen minutes into a walk, she senses a dose of feel-good chemicals. Natural substances such as endorphins shift her mindset. Her thinking becomes clearer. She feels more resilient.

Yes, I am going to ask you about movement. How often do you move your body each week? Are you moving at least fifteen minutes a day? If not, what's keeping you from doing that? If it's pain, your next right action is to figure out the best way to exercise for your body. For example, you could start by looking up "exercises for back pain." You would type in your ailment, of course.

You could also book an appointment with a physical therapist or a yoga therapist. They would help you determine ways that you can move your body without injuring yourself. If you're considering a personal trainer, they need experience with injured clients. Pain is not something you should push through.

Action is a great restorer and builder of confidence.
Inaction is not only the result, but the cause, of fear.

~ Norman Vincent Peale

To create her daily walking habit, Tamara gave herself a sticker on a paper calendar for every walk. The first week was abysmal. She worked two double shifts, and it threw off the entire week. She only got one sticker on her calendar.

Usually, she would give up until work was less hectic, but this time was different. From her reading, she knew that she had a choice. Do it badly, or don't do it at all. She picked badly as her battle cry.

The next week, it was raining most afternoons. She only walked two days. She congratulated herself. After all, she doubled her success in one week. Those three stickers were trophies for her.

The more stickers she amassed on her calendar, the more stickers she wanted to amass. Each walk was a declaration of change. She was taking the fear of not knowing what she wanted to do with her one precious life and shifting gears. Every sticker reinforced the idea that she was on her way to finding out.

With the small success of one and then two and then three weeks of regular exercise, her confidence grew. If she could create a healthy habit like walking daily, what else could she create?

We uncover our nature through action.

~ Steven Pressfield

With a month-long win under her belt, Tamara searched for her next right action. She zigzagged through Houston streets. Her aim was threefold. Get some good exercise. Get to know her city—find her way.

She walked by a home with a kitten warming himself on the windowsill and thought, "Gosh, I miss having a pet." It wasn't a possibility in her apartment. Her roommate was allergic to cats. A few days later, one of her customers mentioned that he volunteers for an animal rescue. She decided to volunteer as a cat socializer.

As she zigzagged through Houston, she also zigzagged her way into homesteading. The animal rescue didn't seem like the place to learn about farming, but it was. She spent most of her time in the cat area but started venturing into helping with other species, too.

The sanctuary was where she met Phil. He was a postman by day and a homesteader by night. Well, really by night and weekends. He grew his own food on his patio in the city but also planted trees on his mom's property outside of the city.

Everyone thought Phil was wild about bunny poo. It's true. He had a homesteading love affair with rabbit feces.

Through Phil, Tamara learned that rabbit poop is the gold standard for manure. Most animal poop is too hot to put directly on plants. We're not talking about temperature here. Hot is the word gardeners use to describe it. The chemical makeup of most fresh manure will burn a plant. It usually needs to break down for a time before it is safe to add to the garden.

Rabbit poo is magical in that you don't need to process it before adding it to your garden. Phil would bring home buckets of rabbit poo from the rescue. He would scatter it throughout his garden.

At the time, this was interesting to Tamara, but she had no real need for it. So, she tucked the knowledge in a mental file and continued with her volunteer work. We'll see later in Tamara's story how that information was useful.

Volunteer work was an interesting mindset shift for her. On a barista's salary, she felt wealthy when she volunteered. She knew that many people couldn't afford an hour a week to sit with cats, but she was lucky to enjoy this time.

She fell in love with George, a big silver cat that hadn't been adopted yet. He had some medical issues, which meant that he might end up living his entire life at the shelter. Her weekly volunteer shifts would always start and end with George.

He loved warming her lap and purring like a wooden roller coaster. Although she couldn't have a cat in her apartment, she was gifted with George every week. He became hers, and she became his.

Looking back, Tamara will tell you that volunteering provided her with numerous gifts. She felt empowered by making the lives of rescue animals a little better. She could clearly see that she enjoyed working with animals. Natural science was a fascinating topic for her. She built a new branch of her community through her weekly volunteering.

Take action every day—some small dose at a time.
\- Jeffrey Gitomer

It was around this time that her next small but significant discovery occurred. She wandered into a farmers' market. You'll remember in chapter two how much she loved the market. It became a weekly routine, too.

Her small doses of action were building a significant life without her planning much.

Buying a small bundle of herbs seems so inconsequential, doesn't it? How on earth could that change someone's life? But it can. And it did.

Aside from feeling like she had a spa in her apartment, the smell of fresh herbs wafting through her room ignited the desire to learn more. She started noticing random questions pop into her mind.

What are the health benefits of lemon balm?

Are there any spiritual properties attributed to rosemary?

What types of folk tales were there about basil?

She replaced her time scrolling through social media with focused time online. She found an app that would offer her distraction-free YouTube. She could find the videos she wanted without getting sucked into clickbait.

Throughout the day, she would jot down the questions that came to her. On weeknights, she allotted thirty minutes for online searching. Those videos and articles answered her questions.

This small action of writing down questions woke up the creative regions of her brain. She started noticing new questions.

What if I grew a few herbs on my windowsill?

What if I cooked with some of the herbs I grew?

When problems arise, new questions form.

I'm running out of windowsill space. What if I found another place to grow food?

*Action breeds confidence and courage. If you want to conquer fear,
do not sit at home and think about it.
Go out and get busy.*

~ Dale Carnegie

Action did, indeed, breed courage for Tamara. Before her first trip to the library, she would never have asked people to help her. Finding an outdoor space for a garden would have been mission impossible. She wouldn't want to be a burden.

After months of small actions, she could see that give and take is essential to a strong community. When she helps animals at the rescue, she feels better about herself. Offering someone the opportunity to help her might give them a sense of usefulness.

Adam Grant's book *Give and Take: Why Helping Others Drives Our Success* gave Tamara new insight. She was beginning to see the interconnectedness of humanity. Rather than seeing her needs as a burden, they could be service opportunities.

With each small success, her confidence grew. She was even able to start seeing failures as learning opportunities. The first time she offered the herbs for sale to a vendor, the person was not interested. She considered this conversation a huge success.

Tamara had never been very good at asking for a fair wage. She always worked at low-paying jobs where asking for a raise was out of the question. Negotiation was a skill she needed to learn.

Asking for more felt uncomfortable. But it was a chance to practice asking for a fair price.

She prepared for the meeting. She called her friend before the initial meeting and shared about her discomfort. Her friend listened and then said, "Me, too! I've been at this job for five years, and the boss has never given me a raise. Asking for more money is so hard. I'm inspired by your willingness to go out there and ask for what you deserve. You can do it!"

After the meeting, she noticed a text from her friend checking in to see how it went. She knew she wasn't doing this all by herself. She had her buddy right there with her. Tamara texted back to tell her it was a huge success. She didn't get the sale, but she did learn how to ask.

Another vendor told her that her price was actually low and that the other vendor didn't have a need for her herbs. From that conversation, she realized that she needed to do more research on the actual price of herbs. This was yet another learning opportunity that empowered her.

It was actions, small and steady ones, that gave Tamara her newfound confidence and courage.

Nothing will work unless you do.

~ Maya Angelou

When Tamara first moved to Houston, she was in a dead-end job with no friends and no interests. She could have easily listed off all the things that were not working in her life.

The heat was wonky in her apartment. She had to wear two layers of clothes to bed on winter nights. There was no room for advancement in her job. She wasn't even interested in advancing there. She had no space to grow food. She ate cheap, overly processed food because that was all she could afford.

She could have easily convinced herself that nothing worked. Instead, she made the conscious decision to make things work and not just work hard at a job she hated like her parents had. She worked to make her life better. Even when she didn't know what that meant, she worked to find out.

And the work wasn't back-breaking, soul-sucking work. It was invigorating. After an exhausting day at the café, she couldn't wait to put her aching feet up with a cup of herbal infusion in hand. Reading about ways to find happiness inspired her. It sure beat watching reruns of a sitcom full of people she'd never meet.

Every day she stepped outside for her walk, she was working for a healthier body and more stable mood. It was work, but the payoff was extraordinary. Nothing worked until she did.

As for the knowledge of rabbit fertilizer, that came in handy when she started gardening in Bao's backyard. She would fertilize her garden with rabbit waste from the animal shelter. She gave a small talk about soil health at the coffeehouse for gardeners. One of the attendees decided to adopt a rabbit from Tamara's animal shelter. So, it was a win-win-win for humans, plants, and a rescue bunny.

Do what you can, with what you have, and do it now!

~ George Washington Carver

Some folks seem to be born with a Do It Now mentality. If that's not you, have no fear. You can foster that character trait. Be like Tamara. Start small. Build on your successes. Do the next indicated action. Do it now.

Your turn, my friend. What are you searching for? Write it down. And write down five actions you can take this week to get closer to your desire. Remember, it doesn't have to be specific when you start. If it's something like "get buff," go a little deeper. What will getting shredded give you? More confidence? More romance? More energy? Your goal can still be to get fit, but you'll have a clearer idea of what you hope to achieve.

I used the Do It Now trick to start this book. My goal was to write the first draft of this book by writing one hour per day with one day off per week. My official start date was November 1.

I started writing two weeks before that date. A soft, early start helped me with motivation. I started with the small success of starting early to create momentum. That action led to the larger success of finishing the first draft.

When I started, I had no idea what the book would look like. I knew that I wanted to write a series of books about how to create a homesteader mindset. What you have in your hands is part one of the series.

I didn't have the book mapped out. I was very unclear about what this book would look like. That might be where you are now. That is totally fine. Insight comes from action.

My pre-start date writing goal was fifteen minutes a day with two days off per week. I told myself that I could write longer, but if I hit fifteen minutes, that was a win. I ended up writing the book outline, book proposal, and chapter one before the start date of November 1. The fifteen minutes easily converted into an hour every morning before my day began.

Shout out to Honorée Corder and Brian Meeks for their book, *The Nifty* 15: *Write Your Book in Just* 15 *Minutes a Day.* FYI: My first book took over eight years to write. So, these authors deserve a huge thank you.

Do It Now worked wonders for me. I had given myself a head start on my lofty goal of finishing a rough draft with a deadline. The first few days were the hardest. I wrestled with thoughts like *Will this be good enough to help others?*

Thankfully, I had the tools to stretch through the discomfort. Before I started typing, I read several books on self-publishing and writing. I immersed myself in the land of writers by listening to podcasts about the art and business of writing.

The one thing that stuck with me from my immersion period was this: Most writers feel a little freaked out when they start a new book. A writer on *The Creative Penn Podcast* said, "I have a sticky note posted to my laptop which says, 'This is the first draft.' My job is to write it. Editing will come later."

When the gremlins pop into my head, I repeat that mantra and keep on typing. My job during the rough draft dash is to write. Not critique. Not modify. Just write.

Well done is better than well said.

~ Benjamin Franklin

I would take ole Ben's adage one step further. Here's my T-shirt quote: "Badly done is better than well said." Once I give myself permission to do something badly, creativity cracks wide open.

Doing something badly is my motto now. I love being the cute foreign chick when I speak French or Spanish or whatever language I'm learning. I'm freaking adorable when I make mistakes. The same is true when I try a new sport. The learning curve is often quite long for me, but who cares? I'm learning. I'm growing. I am more alive.

As for the finished product, that comes in time with effort. I did several revisions to this book. The first was before even my editor saw the rough draft. I enlisted a team of professionals to help me make a viable product.

But I would have never gotten here had I not started with what Anne Lamott calls an SFD: Crappy First Draft. Yes, I know that would be CFD. I'm saving my potty mouth for another day. You can guess what the S stands for.

This book would not exist if it weren't for the wisdom of other writers telling me to "do it now." All the struggles and all the victories are here because I took action. Do it now.

EASY-BREEZY END OF CHAPTER TASKS

- What subject would inspire you to borrow a stack of books? Write that theme or themes in your Homesteader Mindset Journal now.

- How often do you move your body each week? Are you moving at least fifteen minutes a day? If not, what's keeping you from doing that?

- What are you searching for? Write it down. And write down five actions you can take this week to get closer to your desire. Do one of those actions right now.

PART THREE

THREE MYTHS TO DECONSTRUCT

But...But...But...

Me, too. I've let a mess of stinky buts stop me from living the dream throughout my life. I'd like to write a book, but I don't have time. I want to start a new career, but it's too complicated. It would be great to speak another language, but I wouldn't know where to start.

Once I deconstructed those myths, I was able to do remarkable things. I mean, look at me! I wrote a book. I'm still amazed at that. And you can be amazed at your accomplishments, too.

In part three of this book, we're going to kick those buts to the curb. We're putting on our myth-busters uniforms. We are scouring the dark corners of our minds that hold fear of making terrible mistakes.

Do you want to know a secret about terrible mistakes? As long as it's not something that could cause physical harm, mistakes are not so terrible. They are a part of being seen—a part of truly living.

There are a million and one myths that the mind can cook up. We're going to focus on the three biggies. Lack of time. Lack of money. Too much complexity.

And trust me when I tell you that I've danced with these myths time and again. Even though I'm more courageous than I've ever been in my life, fear gives me a creepy hug every now and again. So, you're not alone. We are in this together. And the solutions are available right now.

CHAPTER 8

I DON'T HAVE TIME TO MAKE POSITIVE CHANGES

"I don't have time to make positive changes." This was a precious myth to Sara. She believed it religiously. She had a mental altar constructed in her mind. There, she bowed down to the god of "I don't have time" every morning before she got out of bed.

It was an exhausting way to live. Sara thought she had found the answer to "not enough time." She would work twelve- to fourteen-hour shifts five days a week and have weekends off to recover. Her husband couldn't understand why she needed to work such long hours. With a huge workload and an even bigger mortgage, Sara thought this was the only option.

Ever since she could remember, she's wanted to be the change she wishes to see in the world. Help others. And spend more time being a part of the solution. She was doing that in her professional life as a social worker. However, making changes at home always seemed like an impossible mission.

She didn't know how to cook. That didn't matter because she didn't have the energy to cook. Most of their meals were packaged goods like takeout. Every time she opened a plastic bag of lettuce, she would wince. She knew that with each meal, she was creating excess waste. Her family wasn't getting the nutrients they needed with fast food, and that bothered her a great deal. But she just didn't have time to make a change.

Her two days off to rest were filled with household responsibilities. She was the official taxi for her boys, and they were involved in a number of extracurricular activities. Busy was the family motto.

In response to a question about how she was doing, Sara would routinely reply, "I'm busy but good." She was often on the go. At times, her body would revolt, and she'd be laid up with the flu. Otherwise, she was running.

The only problem was she was running on empty. One morning, it all stopped. She woke up tired that morning and felt sleepy as she began her drive. She dropped the kids off at school and was making her way to the office when she stopped at a busy intersection to wait for the left arrow to turn green.

She saw the color green and started to turn. Seconds later, she was hit by another car speeding toward her at fifty miles per hour. Sara had made a left turn when she saw the green light for traffic going straight. The other car collided with hers and pushed her vehicle into a telephone pole.

Sara doesn't remember the rest of the accident, but she learned later that the person in the other car was unharmed. It was a different story for Sara. She was found unconscious with several broken bones and a traumatic brain injury. Sara was lucky to be alive.

After sixteen days in the hospital, Sara was released into her husband's care. Her bones were mending, but her brain needed rest. Her doctor gave her instructions to remain on medical leave until her head injury healed.

Initially, this was an easy task as Sara was too weak and nauseous to want to do anything other than sleep. As she began to walk again, she felt the urge to be useful. She was raised in a household where you pay your way. Being a productive human was her life purpose.

How could she lie there when her family and work needed her?

It was this question that plagued her. She felt like every day of rest was a waste. Although her responsibility was to heal, she had a long list of tasks that needed to be completed. One day, she had a meltdown. She told her husband that she felt lost. He listened quietly. Then he simplified the solution. Sara had only three tasks on her list during her recovery period.

Eat.

Rest.

Poop.

He continued to explain this list. If she checked each of these off each day, she could consider herself a success. Everything else would either be handled by him or her health care team or it would be postponed. When she was healthy enough to handle a task, she could try it again.

But for now, eat-rest-poop was the goal.

For the first time in her life, Sara relaxed. She had a plan. It was ridiculously simple. More importantly, she knew that it was time to trust the process.

Sara and Jim had been married for ten years at that time. She knew that she could trust him to make sure the kids were being taken care of. He was a master at boundary setting and getting adequate rest. It was her time to learn the art of letting go.

Sara's workaholic lifestyle died a slow death during her recovery. Her essential tasks were either handled by someone else. Or they weren't as important as she thought they were. This was both freeing and frustrating. She wasn't integral to making the world keep spinning. Who knew!?

It was freeing because this realization opened a chasm of options. If she didn't have to do all the things she thought were necessary, what would she do with her time? How could she create a life that aligned with her values?

It was frustrating. Sara could easily convince herself that she had wasted thirty-plus years spinning out. During dark moments, she wrestled with this idea. She used this feeling of loss to motivate her to make uncomfortable changes.

The words of her pastor echoed in her mind. "So what? Now what?" She mentally brushed herself off. "Okay, so what? I have behaviors that have wasted time. Now what? What do I do about it?" The first thing she did was get some help with those habits.

There was some extra time during her eat-rest-poop routine, but she wasn't interested in filling it up with nonsense. She decided that her biggest issue was not having enough time.

Sara pondered this. Other women had similar responsibilities. They were able to take time for healthy choices and even self-care. Maybe they knew something that she didn't.

Her head injury made it difficult to read for long periods of time. Extensive reading was not an option. She started her time management quest with friends who would visit her. Asking the cooks in her life how they learned to cook was her first step. Then she asked how they fit healthy meals into their busy lives.

There were some surprising discoveries. One of her friends only spends one two-hour session a week on meal prep. This friend would make one big batch meal like chicken rice soup.

She would double the batch and freeze the extra servings. Et voilà! Her family now had a home-cooked meal and several "fast-food" servings for the following weeks.

Another friend spilled her secret. "You have no idea how easy it is to whip up a good meal with olive oil, salt, and pepper. I can show you if you'd like." She offered to teach Sara how to cook meals that took ten minutes to make. The secret was keeping your pantry stocked with whole foods that are easy to prepare.

On each visit, they would catch up on life while making a simple meal for Sara's family. With a little planning, she can now make a healthy meal in less time than ordering takeout.

This same friend taught her the art of empowering her children to cook for the family, too. This gave the boys hands-on learning opportunities. It also took the burden off Sara for every single meal. She was surprised to see how much her sons enjoyed the chance to create a meal from start to finish.

She knew that having fresh veggies was going to add nutrient density to her family's diet. So, she used her once-a-week batch cooking to add a task. She and her sons spent thirty minutes chopping up fresh veggies. The vegetables were then stored in glass containers in the fridge. With a shake of salt and a drizzle of olive oil, a side of roasted veggies was ready for every meal.

Moving from plastic packages to glass containers gave her inspiration. Sara found other ways to reduce their household waste. There was a grocery store that sold grains in bulk. She took her large mason jars to the store in place of using plastic bags. Buying in bulk saved them money and kept their trash can from filling up.

Sara was recovering from a broken leg. So, she had to find ways to make traditional cooking easy on her body. She used a stool to sit on while chopping veggies and stood with one foot raised on the lowest bar of the stool to help her back while washing dishes.

These activities were painful at times. She learned how to take lots of breaks. Walking away for a nap mid-task was something she had to practice while healing. She set phone alarms at 11:30 a.m., 2:30 p.m., and 5:30 p.m. to remind her that it might be time to lie down for a rest.

When her nap alarm went off, she reminded herself of her top three priorities. Her new mantra became "If I eat, rest, and poop today, I am a success." The more she recovered, the more she was able to enjoy the process of rebuilding her life.

Even then, she kept busy days simple. She had a handyman working around her house one day. She told herself, *Not much is going to get done with the commotion and decisions that need to be made on the repairs. It is okay if I don't get a lot checked off my list today. I will lower my expectations to making a batch of beef stew and managing my handy helper.* Sara ended up getting a few small tasks checked off her list, but they were bonuses. The real success was that her stress level was manageable. Her daily recovery goal taught her to pare things back.

Each night she and Jim would dream together of ways to create more of the homesteader mindset they both craved. It was Jim who came up with the idea of moving into a smaller house. He wanted to create more space in their budget for less work outside the home and more free time for them.

Each time her family sat around the dinner table and enjoyed a meal together, her confidence grew. Dinners were filled with moments of genuine laughter, and she wanted more. Cooking was the first step in Jim and Sara's homesteading journey.

She could have her homemade cake and eat it, too.

Her company was patient as she recovered, but they had their limitations. When she requested a return to the office part-time, her boss wasn't as flexible as she'd hoped. Instead, she found another part-time job in her field. It was an act of faith to change companies, but it ended up working out well for her.

You are probably thinking right now, "Well, that's all fine and good. But I don't plan on having a near-death experience anytime soon. So, how do I create more time?" Hold your horses. I'm not finished with the story.

Jim was affected by Sara's accident, too.

Suddenly, he had double the work on top of his worry for Sara's well-being. The first month or so, he let everything go to Hades in a handbasket. It was all he could do to keep the boys fed and get to work on time.

A few friends offered to help, but he didn't have the time or energy to delegate. It was only when their dear friend, Pammie, offered to organize that he relaxed enough to accept help. Pammie knew that Jim and Sara had their hands full.

She wrote up a list of things she guessed that Sara and Jim might need. Her list included things like paying the bills, washing dishes, doing a load of laundry, and taking Sara to appointments.

Next, she took the list to Sara and asked her whether she was on the right track. Sara added a few things to the wish list, like taking the boys to sports practice.

Pammie put her project manager cap on and devised a schedule of events and chores. She called a list of friends, family, and church members that Jim provided and asked for their help. When she reached someone who was available to help, she would email them a sign-up sheet for the chores.

Pammie signed herself up to do dishes and a load of laundry every Wednesday at lunchtime. Five people signed up to help with the list of chores. Most of them arrived at the same hour each week so that Jim could plan their days around the helper visits.

Jim's first success in creating positive change was accepting help from his community. He was proud of the fact that he could provide for his family, but this tragedy was too much for him to handle on his own.

The next thing he did was begin to habit stack his positive changes. Habit stack is a term that author James Clear explains in *Atomic Habits*. It was one of the first books Sara listened to while she was recovering. She explained the concept to Jim over breakfast, and he decided to give it a try.

Instead of creating a new habit willy-nilly, you stack your new habit next to a habit that already exists. Jim had the established habit of watching the news before bed. He added a new habit to his existing routine. While watching the news, he would do one household chore that needed tending. He could watch the news and fold laundry or pack up tomorrow's lunch.

During his lunch hour, Jim usually sat at his desk. He would eat while watching something online. He added a habit stack to this routine, too.

He started to take a thirty-minute walk at lunchtime. A boost of energy from exercise was perfect for midday. He also had time to make personal calls regarding Sara's health care and the boys' activities. He rewarded himself with his usual lunch routine for the remaining thirty minutes.

His lunchtime viewing started to shift. Jim was blown away by how a simple home-cooked meal could beat restaurant fare in a contest of taste. He found a few YouTube cooking channels. Because his son Zach had taken a liking to cooking, Jim often sent videos to him. They discussed what their new cooking adventure would be.

During the second month of Sara's recovery, Jim found a two-hour cooking class in a neighboring town. He and Zach attended as a father/son excursion. It was a great way to get their minds off the heaviness of their home situation. Having something scheduled into his week was another way to make space. Jim wanted more quality time with his sons. He also knew a night of fun distraction would help Zach.

They ended up bringing home the dessert they made for Sara and Matthew. Sara joked that she wanted them to take more classes that involved dessert making.

Jim knew that his youngest son, Matthew, needed attention during this time, too. So, they came up with a plan to make a bookshelf for Sara out of old wine crates. It was a fairly easy project involving nails and a few free wine crates from their local wine store.

The bookshelf took them about an hour to create, and Matthew couldn't wait to show his mom what he'd made her. It gave him satisfaction to do something nice for her during her healing period. This was another appointment that Jim had scheduled into his day planner.

Matthew really took to making things out of reused material. With his dad's help, he picked up a few more wine crates and built himself a desk. Jim was impressed by how handy his son was becoming. He was also relieved to see Matthew working for stretches of time without checking his phone.

Jim knew that buying a smaller house was a task that would take a good deal of time. He dedicated his morning commute to interviewing real estate agents over the phone. When he found a good fit, he called her every morning on the drive to work to see what new inventory she had found. He also blocked out Saturday mornings for house shopping, and that included discussing the next steps with Sara and their realtor.

He relished lazy Sunday mornings when he could sleep in and give their boys full reign of the kitchen. A Sunday morning rest was a luxury. He stayed in bed with Sara, and they snuggled.

Jim's Saturday morning work soon paid off, and the couple were successful at locating a new home that was less expensive. And, once they moved, Jim had his Saturdays back. He used this already established routine to habit stack something new. He was used to sitting down for two to four hours of work, and he wanted to begin using that time for another useful project. He didn't want to lose his momentum.

Jim thought it might be a good idea to use that time to bring some of their daydreams to fruition. He started by working on finding a solution to his long commute. He loved his job, but the sixty-minute commute ate up two hours every weekday. After breakfast on Saturdays, he was committed to looking for a job closer to home. Within four weeks, he had three comparable jobs that were located within fifteen miles of his house. He couldn't believe that one hour a week of job searching had offered that many options.

After careful consideration, Jim decided on a job that was a mere ten-minute drive from his house. He had just found one hundred extra minutes per day with his job change. Once again, he didn't want to lose momentum. So, he allotted that found time to homesteading and self-development.

He continued to wake up and get ready for work at the same time as he did for his old job. Being a night owl, he knew that his most productive fifty-minute session would be after work. He used his fifty minutes before the start of his day to do tasks that didn't involve a great deal of thinking. That was when he would tackle his don't-really-want-to-do-it list.

For the first two months, he used a timer to sort boxes of stuff in the garage. Because Sara was recovering during their move, Jim moved the boxes from one garage to the next. He had no idea what was in them. He intuitively knew that getting rid of clutter would create more space for his family—both physically and mentally.

Sara was not well enough to help with the garage organization. So, Jim decided to create a pile that Sara could review once a week. It would take her ten minutes to tell him what could go and what needed to stay. (This could also work for the spouse who doesn't think cleaning the garage is important.)

Some mornings, Jim would only have enough willingness to set his timer for fifteen minutes. More often than not, he would find motivation during those first fifteen minutes, and he would often continue cleaning for another thirty minutes.

It's amazing how much can be done, even in short sessions. Before long, the garage was organized, and they knew where everything was as it was labeled. He'd also made room for a work area for Matthew to continue his woodworking projects.

After the satisfaction of creating usable storage space in the garage, Jim continued the morning sessions. He was checking off tasks like fixing wobbly doorknobs, and completing those small things was gratifying.

Before we continue with the story, you might be shaking your head in disbelief. Maybe you're a single parent. Maybe you're struggling financially. If so, I recommend reading *The Successful Single Mom* by Honorée Corder. Her tips can help you find ways to support positive change.

Okay. Back to Jim and Sara.

As Sara got better, she was inspired by Jim's progress. Cleaning little forgotten piles of books and papers tucked away in corners of the house was easy. Her sessions were five minutes at a time during her recovery, but those five minutes were glorious. During months of recovery, she felt happy to be making progress on things that had been ignored for years.

After work, Jim wanted to use his additional fifty minutes for self-development. He created a habit stack with his ten-minute commute home from work. Each weekday, he stopped to have a coffee at the locally owned coffeehouse. He ordered a three-dollar coffee and chatted with the staff for a few minutes.

Fifteen dollars for weekday coffee was well within his budget. Since he was packing healthy lunches, he saved double that amount on fast food runs. When he needed to tighten his belt, he cut his expenses elsewhere. The three-dollar fee was his rent for a brainstorming space.

Having social interaction and a community connection gave his extroverted personality energy. He usually made his way to his favorite chair and pulled out a notebook and pen. At times, he simply wrote a list of what he thought would be needed for his next project. Other times, he listened to a homesteading podcast about a topic he was considering. He took notes about ideas he wanted to remember.

One of his first projects was learning to raise chickens for fresh eggs. He started by telling his friend from church, Brian, about his desire to raise chickens. Brian, a backyard gardener, was interested in helping Jim with this project because he wanted to learn how to do it himself. They met every Tuesday afternoon at the coffeehouse to plan their project together. Jim found himself looking forward to weekly chats with Brian.

Once they had the plans ready, they scheduled two Saturdays in a row. They were going to build the coop and chicken tractor with their children. Sara and Brian's wife cooked a huge lunch for everyone on both days. It was more of a party than a project.

Jim's fifty-minute after-work brainstorming drastically changed his life for the better. We'll talk a bit more about using found time in chapter twelve. You, my friend, are more than ready to drastically change your life for the better. Let's look at some reflection questions before we press on.

EASY-BREEZY END OF CHAPTER TASKS

- What are five habits you do every single day without fail? They don't have to be positive habits. If the first thing you do every morning before getting out of bed is check your phone, that's a very strong habit to stack. Write it down.

- Think for a moment and write down five habits you wish you had in your life. Write at least one for each aspect of life: emotional, mental, physical, spiritual. Here are a few examples.

  - Emotional: Five-minute guided meditation on joy

  - Mental: Learn to play piano in ten minutes a day

  - Physical: Start a one-minute yoga habit

  - Spiritual: Write a five-sentence prayer to your higher power

- Did you notice that each of my examples is only a few minutes long? That's because starting small is a great way to build on your success. Pick one of your old habits in item one and habit stack one of your desired habits from item two. Commit to making this a habit for thirty days. Start it today. We'll talk more about growing that habit in part four.

CHAPTER 9

A HOMESTEADER MINDSET IS ONLY FOR LUCKY RICH PEOPLE

A homesteader mindset is only for the rich. As author Byron Katie, would say, "Is it true? Can you prove that that statement is true?"

Being a barista gives Tamara enough income to pay her bills. She's excellent at her job. It offers her freedom from thinking about work after hours. Her boss and colleagues are pleasant. It's work, but it's not the worst gig.

However, she doesn't have money for her dream of homesteading. According to the US Department of Labor, Tamara is a member of the working poor class. She doesn't own land. There are no shopping sprees at the bookstore or expensive homestead courses at a local farm. Her budget doesn't have room for those things.

She uses her time and creativity to get what she needs for her homesteading journey. She considers every little thing she's doing to be her formal education. Libraries. Gardening in her neighbor's yard. Vermicomposting and volunteer work. These activities fill up her free time.

I deliberately used the hot potato word "poor" when introducing Tamara in chapter two. It's a weighted word. Especially when you use it in the term "working poor." The word "poor" has a number of meanings. One definition is having a lower income. Another is used to describe a lesser quality. And yet another suggested that poor means the person should be pitied. Wow. The combination of those three meanings really is a hot potato.

If you asked her, Tamara would tell you that she fit into only one of those categories. She is living below the poverty level. She considered herself rich in qualities that helped her live a homesteader mindset. We'll talk about those qualities in this chapter.

After reading *One-Straw Revolutionary*, Tamara could clearly see that she was not the only one. The author, Larry Korn, detailed the life of Masanobu Fukuoka. That Japanese farmer bucked the system.

Many chose to live below the poverty level with substantial lives. They ate well. They had strong community ties. They enjoyed lots of free time. They were healthy and content. What's poor about that?

As for "lesser quality," Tamara uses a daily practice of gratitude to keep her outlook bright. The act of gratitude was initially something she learned from her first-generation parents. They immigrated to the United States ten years before Tamara was born. No matter how little they had, they focused on whatever abundance was available to them.

Their story was one of many from their native country. Her parents lost their small farm when it was seized by a tyrannical government. They could have wallowed in the atrocities that they experienced. Instead, they used the practice of gratitude to keep afloat. Her father would stop their car to enjoy a sunset with his children. Her mother would touch the heads of her babies and thank God for their health. Gratitude was a way of life for them.

Tamara took this practice with her. Because she enjoys journaling, she uses a few minutes each day to write a gratitude list. She keeps her gratitude journal where she can reach it when she wakes up.

In times of trouble, she writes an extra gratitude list. When she has a hard time focusing, she makes a list of items starting from A to Z. Apples are often top of the list because she loves homemade applesauce.

It's super easy to make. I've included a recipe for apple compote at the back of this book. I'm pretty sure it will make it onto your gratitude list as well.

Tamara attributes her ability to weather emotional storms as a gift that she was given. Her practice of gratitude affords her an instant attitude adjustment. Yes, her balanced mind is a gift, but it's one that she worked to develop.

And it's not limited to her journaling sessions. She plays the grateful game when she's looking for a parking spot. She lists out loud all the things she's grateful for at that moment. The winner is the item she mentioned when she found an open spot. She considers that a spotlight of grace. A little "look at this great thing" message.

If she needs a pick-me-up during a difficult period, she will sometimes call a close friend. If she gets voicemail, she'll leave a message listing a few of the things she's grateful for. It's normal for her and her friends to swap messages and texts with lists of gratitude.

Let's look at some character traits Tamara has developed living a homesteader mindset with a low-income job.

COURAGE

It takes a great deal of courage for a person to step out of their comfort zone and try something new—even if their comfort zone is uncomfortable. Tamara considers herself lucky. Her level of internal discomfort was just high enough to motivate her to change.

She didn't have to have Joan of Arc's courage. All she needed was the willingness to take the next right action. In her case, walking into the public library and walking out with a book was her first courageous step.

In some cases, an act of courage must be done numerous times. A battered woman will, on average, attempt to leave a violent relationship seven times before successfully ending the relationship.

This is an extreme example, but it's worth noting that even the most courageous acts don't happen overnight. Each thought of change is a step in the right direction. In the case of a person leaving an unhealthy relationship, it often requires a plan.

TENACITY (PERSISTENCE)

I like the word "tenacity." It stings a little when I say it. The spicy syllables come out of my mouth, daring me to stop them. That's the beauty of tenacity and its softer-sounding sister, persistence.

Tamara isn't outwardly tenacious. She is quietly stubborn. When someone scoffs and tells her that one of her plans is outrageous, she smiles and asks them why. She listens intently to their reasons and takes mental notes.

The naysayers give her ample material for planning. Someone complained that her house would be filled with gnats. So, she researched what aspects of indoor gardening attracted gnats. Then she avoided those conditions.

Don't get the wrong idea. She became disheartened with her plans from time to time. Her first attempt at lacto-fermentation pickled onions ended up slimy and gross. She hated losing two onions in the process.

Instead of giving up, she cleaned up. She stopped by Bao's yard and buried the gunk into a small compost hole in her garden. Then she went home and tried again. This time she didn't stray from the directions. A week later, she had happy probiotic-filled onions for her salads.

What is lacto-fermentation? It's the most nutrient-dense type of pickling you can do. It's easy, too. And you know me by now. Easy and fun are my top two priorities in creating a homesteader mindset.

Most pickling from stores is done with unfermented vinegar. This doesn't give you as many health benefits as homemade fermented pickling. Pickled veggies made with lacto-fermentation create natural probiotics that support your gut health. Eating fermented veggies aids in proper digestion, blood sugar stabilization, weight loss, and even mood lift.

The other great reason to make fermented pickled veggies at home? It's freaking delish! After eating beet greens for weeks, I pull out two beets, a few carrots, and an onion from my garden. Once pickled with beets, the pink onion slices remind me of hoagie toppings from my childhood. The red carrots are a great way to enjoy a probiotic snack during the day. It's also a unique gift to give when you are invited to a dinner party. People love homemade goodies.

It takes me a grand total of ten minutes to wash, chop, and prepare the pickling. All you need is salt, water, a jar with a tight lid, and a little time. I watched a lot of instructional videos on it. Some folks make it more complicated than necessary. I've compiled a list of easy-to-do, easy-to-understand videos for you, my beloved reader.

Visit: www.createwellnessproject.com/bookbonus.

CURIOSITY

Tamara was a curious child. She would spend hours outside watching nature with wonder. She loved how ants organize their daily work. Pondering the tiny streams that form after a rainfall was a favorite pastime.

She doesn't need to know every detail about how things work. Her enjoyment comes from discovery through observation. The character asset of curiosity didn't leave her when she entered adulthood.

She turned her observant nature to the study of humans. Most specifically, her customers at the coffeehouse. As she was reading about happiness, Tamara began to wonder, *What makes my typically happy clients so content? What is their secret?*

As she read about methods for a more homesteader mindset, she began to ask her happy clients questions. What are your hobbies? What do you love about your job? How did you know your spouse was the one? These are simple questions. Ones that can be asked in the middle of a slow day at the coffeehouse without seeming like more than small talk.

With answers from her customers, she looked inward with similar questions. What seems like a fun hobby for me? What do I love about my job? What do I envision a loving relationship would be for me?

Tamara uses her curiosity to build a foundation for her homesteader mindset.

FAITH

Faith means a lot of things to a lot of people. Some would define it as trust in something or someone. Others would describe faith as a religious belief or spiritual philosophy. For Tamara, it is a mix.

She strongly believes that people are mostly good. She has faith in the goodwill of humankind. This doesn't mean that she puts herself in danger by meeting "good people" in a dark alley to buy a watch. It means that, all in all, she made the decision to believe that most people wanted peace just like her.

This trust in the good of humankind allows her more opportunities to expand her community. She isn't afraid to ask others for help or advice. She knows that offering an opportunity for someone to be of service is also a gift. That's how she views her garden barter with Bao. She is not only paying her with fresh produce but also offering Bao the opportunity to be of service.

Faith is a muscle for Tamara. She must exercise her faith every day. Her daily list of gratitude reminds her of all the goodness she has already received. That helps her grow her faith that all will be well in her future.

She also dedicates time for prayer before every meal she has at home. It isn't hours of prayer, but it adds up to a lovely connection with her higher power. During prayer, she thanks God for the nourishment that the food is bringing her. She gives thanks for her family and friends. She asks for blessings for the helpers in her life, and for those she knows are going through a hard time as well the oppressed and the oppressors of the world.

For her, building faith is something that utilizes her past, present, and future. She looks to her past to remind her of the hard times that she survived. "If I could get through that, I can handle this," is something she often tells herself.

Her daily prayers and meditations are part of her action plan to build faith. She started the practice of meditation by listening to a five-minute meditation on her phone. She uses the free app Insight Timer.

From there, she built her meditation practice to twenty minutes daily. Much of the time, the last five minutes of her daily walks are dedicated to meditation. She will count her steps or repeat a phrase in time with her breath. Her favorite phrase to repeat is "Thank you."

Meditation is a practice that she cherishes. It is her listening time. She is quieting the mind of clutter to make room for more new, positive thoughts.

Faith isn't something that comes easily to Tamara. Because she read that faith was an important aspect of happiness, she decided to make it a goal. She even tried out a few different places of worship to see whether one of them was a fit for her.

GENEROSITY

Tamara was raised in a culture of kindness. When her immigrant parents were living hand to mouth, there was always space at the table for one more. There were times in her childhood when someone was living in her family's home because they didn't have a place to go.

Her father taught her that sharing is a way to create wealth. It might not be the type of wealth that immediately comes to mind. He wasn't talking about big piles of gold. He was talking about universal reciprocity.

Well, that's a big term to chew up and swallow, isn't it? Reciprocity means mutual exchange of goods.

In the case of Tamara's garden, Bao rents Tamara space in her backyard. Tamara pays Bao with vegetables she grows in the garden.

But there's something even bigger here. Universal means relating to all beings. Tamara knows that each time she gives of herself, generosity comes back to her tenfold.

Every time she spends an hour in the cat sanctuary, she grows her universal reciprocity account. She also receives instant gratification in the form of purrs and snuggles.

She is on the lookout for gratitude. Tamara is always looking to see where her acts of kindness are coming back to her and in what form. If a friend buys her lunch, she considers that an act of kindness. She writes it down in her gratitude journal that evening.

When her volunteer buddy gave her a bucket of compost, that was a result of universal reciprocity. She needn't give Phil anything in return. She simply pays it forward by sharing a jar of her freshly dried rosemary with a neighbor who loves to cook.

Because of her gratitude practice, she can clearly see all the wealth she has to share.

CREATIVITY

Of all her attributes, creativity is the one that Tamara holds dear. While she does do things that people see as creative, she also values creativity in daily life. For example, she likes to knit small toys for her nieces and nephews. That activity falls squarely into the creativity sector. She values her time knitting on a park bench.

However, she values her creative spirit in all aspects of her life. One of her most creative endeavors is pondering. She'll think up something she would love to do. Then she'll spend little bits of quiet time dreaming up how to do it. Sometimes, she'll merely contemplate what the activity will look like for her.

Pondering is something that people might not exactly consider a creative project. The planning phases of her goals are some of the most exciting times for Tamara. She doesn't stop at the planning phase. She takes the next small action toward the goal. Then she continues to enjoy a dip from time to time in the vast pool of her active imagination.

Certain visualizations come to fruition rather clearly. She had been envisioning spending time on a farm. She could see herself in her black T-shirt and jeans. She imagined walking down a wooded path with a beautiful barn on her right side.

One day, she found herself dressed as she imagined with a barn to her right while walking on a wooded path. It was the farm where she started volunteering one weekend per month. She was elated to see the power of her creativity at work.

EASY-BREEZY END OF CHAPTER TASKS

- Write one to three sentences about a time in your life when you possessed each of these character assets.
  - Courage
  - Tenacity
  - Faith
  - Generosity
  - Creativity

- Write down one way that you can express these positive qualities in your life this very week.
  - Courage
  - Tenacity
  - Faith
  - Generosity
  - Creativity

- Schedule time into your day tomorrow to focus on doing something with one of these qualities. It can be as short as two minutes.

CHAPTER 10

IT IS TOO COMPLICATED

One of the biggest myths regurgitated is "[Some task] is too complicated." When I give someone a tour of my compost piles, they are often impressed with how nice they smell. And my gardening friends do cartwheels when I give them a bucket of black gold. Then they shake their heads and say, "I would love to do this, but it's just too complicated."

This myth seeps into much of what people want to do but never get around to actually doing. It's sad, really. People are putting off their dreams because they think it's too complicated. That happened to Mitch and Lucy.

Mitch is the official king of all things practical in his family. He loves finding thrifty ways to make use of things that are destined for the trash can. When he was working, he saved paper from the printer to use for printing on the other side. He put a box next to the printer. Every bit of scrap paper that still had one blank side would find its way face down into the box. This was back in the '90s when recycling wasn't as easy to do. He was so very proud of his ability to get two printed pages for the price of one.

In retirement, he turned his focus to things in his home that were destined for the trash can. While sliding the remains of his salad into a trash can one day, a lightbulb went off. The leaves of lettuce could be used to feed the worms in his garden. But how?

He was bitten by the composting bug. Mitch couldn't wait to start a compost pile. He found a local compost class and signed up. To his dismay, Lucy was not enthusiastic. "I don't want maggots in my yard." She had heard that maggots live in compost piles, and she wanted nothing to do with it.

There are ways to eliminate the possibility of those white wiggly things in your compost. I'll get to that in a bit. For now, just know that Lucy was no fan of composting.

One dull lecture about composting was enough to squash the composting bug in Mitch. The long thermometer and precise temperatures that the instructor described seemed too complicated. Mitch's eyes glazed over more than once at the charts about nitrogen and carbon. He left the class feeling deflated.

As mentioned earlier, Mitch bought a little book titled *Compost Everything* by David The Good. This book was exactly what Lucy needed. It was humorous. It was short. It was very, very simple. One day, she went out to the garden and surprised Mitch by setting up their first compost pile.

The secret to Lucy's enthusiasm was that David The Good made composting simple. He reminded her that things rot and break down in nature without a thermometer and charts. David gave Lucy permission to take the easy way.

Lucy created her first pile behind their garage where it wouldn't be seen. It was super simple. She tied some chicken wire into a large cylinder using zip ties. Then she put some vegetable scraps from her trash at the bottom of the pile. After that, she spread dry grass clippings on top.

She learned from David The Good that if food is covered with a brown layer such as dry clippings, flies will not lay eggs. Hence, the nightmarish maggot fear was gone.

The flip to this part of their story is that Lucy is now the compost queen of their family. Through experimentation, she's managed to create a very easy composting system. So easy that I'd be remiss if I didn't describe it to you.

Let's walk you through the journey of Lucy's food from kitchen to compost to garden.

SIMPLE COMPOSTING SYSTEM

After she chops up vegetables, Lucy walks the scraps over to the freezer. They are deposited into a biodegradable shopping bag. Why the freezer? She tried having the compost scraps on the counter, but she didn't like the gnats that circled around the bins. Even the special compost containers with gnat-resistant filters on top didn't work for her. She had a little extra space in the freezer and took advantage of it.

Once a week, she takes her frozen scraps and dumps them into the compost pile. She takes a few handfuls of dry grass clippings and adds a layer of them to the pile. Then she steps back to admire how high her compost pile is growing. Lastly, Lucy saunters back to the house to finish her morning coffee.

And it's done. Seriously, that's it. She doesn't turn it. She does water it when she thinks it looks too dry. But the rest is up to nature.

She filled the compost pile up to the top and simply started a new one while the first one cooked. In seven months, she noticed that her first pile was starting to shrink. According to what she read about compost piles, she knew that meant that it was beginning to break down.

About nine months in, she got impatient and lifted the chicken wire up to investigate. Inside the bottom of the pile was moist, black compost. To her, it looked and smelled exactly like what her garden store was selling. She was so excited! She shoveled out the black gold and put the rest back into the pile for further cooking.

Lucy had plenty of room behind her garage for creating numerous compost piles. She usually had four. One that was being built slowly. And three that were cooking at different stages.

But what if you don't have room for four compost piles? What if you don't have room in your freezer for a food scrap bag? It's still a simple system that just needs to be tweaked a little.

SMALL SPACE COMPOSTING

When her daughter took an interest in creating a compost pile, she asked Lucy for help. Her daughter didn't have a lot of space to create four big piles. She had just enough room behind her tool shed for one main pile. She and Lucy were determined to figure out an easy compost plan that would work.

They used a different method for the initial scraps. Lucy's daughter didn't have room in her freezer for a bag of food scraps. So, her dad made a container for under the sink. It was a plastic coffee container with a resealable lid. This became a food scrap container for his daughter.

Mitch bought a charcoal filter in the kitty litter section of a nearby pet store. After drilling five air holes in the lid, he superglued the filter to the underside of the lid. This keeps odors to a minimum and doesn't let gnats know where the scrap stash is.

Outside, Lucy's daughter made one big compost pile and one small starter pile. They measured out a 4x4 square against her concrete privacy wall. The square was lined on two sides with cinder blocks. So, it was a three-sided area with one open side.

The layering is very similar. Lucy's daughter has a lot of shredded paper from the office. She uses some of that for her brown layer. Her kids dump the kitchen scraps into the pile and layer it with a mixture of shredded paper and dry leaves.

Dry leaves need to be chopped up, as whole ones take longer to break down. Running the lawnmower over a pile of leaves will do the trick. They chop up a bunch of leaves and store them in a trash can. That way, it is ready whenever needed.

This is a compact setup. They have one compost pile, one container of brown material, and another pile to start as the first one cooks.

Because they only have one pile, they need to cook it faster. Every two weeks, Lucy's daughter turns the compost pile. It is about a thirty-minute chore and good exercise. She takes a pitchfork and moves the pile out of its cooking spot. As she moves it, she gently breaks up any clumps that aren't breaking down. She then puts the turned pile back in its cooking spot. Every now and then, she uses a watering can to moisten the pile as she puts it back. In about a month or two, her pile is fully cooked. Lucy's daughter is elated.

A few things surprised Lucy and her daughter about this process. They couldn't believe how nice the pile smelled while breaking down. There were no flies. There was no stink of rotting food. When her daughter turned it, the smell was very similar to a walk in the woods.

Another surprise was the life inside the pile. Once earthworms and grubs find their way there, the composting happens rather quickly. Both Lucy and her daughter foster this relationship. They leave a thin layer of the original compost to start her new pile.

The compost critters, like worms and grubs, work night and day to shrink the compost pile. It seems like overnight the pile is six inches shorter from the little Pac-Mans. Those critters munch their way through celery bits and mango pits.

SIFTING COMPOST

Both Lucy and her daughter use the same process of sifting. This is how to move completed compost into a container for use in the garden. A compost sifter is a simple instrument made with ¼ inch mesh wire and four wood or metal sides. It looks like a shallow, square bowl with a mesh bottom—much like the characters panning for gold in the movies.

To use a sifter, put a few handfuls of compost on it and run your fingers through the pile. Completed compost falls through the mesh. The bigger pieces still need more time to break down.

Sifting through the completed compost pile is Lucy's favorite part of the process. She turns a bucket upside down to use as her seat, and hand sifts the pile into a large container. She bought a handmade sifter on Etsy from a nearby vendor.

A word about Etsy. It's still online shopping, but you have the option to select vendors in your state or your country. This cuts down on the carbon load while supporting small handcraft businesses. It's where I shop when I want to skip big chains but can't seem to find what I need in local stores.

Okay. Where were we in the story? Oh, right. The joy of sifting!

The bigger pieces and grubs go back into the new compost pile. Lucy enjoys touching the completed compost with her bare hands. It is as near to a spiritual experience as she's ever had.

There she sits on her upside-down bucket in awe of the regenerative power of nature. All these years, she felt terrible about adding to landfills. All the worry about depleted soil had taken its toll on her spirit. And there, in that tiny corner of the universe, she is grateful to take part in a beautiful, closed loop.

WHAT IS A CLOSED LOOP?

Closed-loop gardening is a method of reusing and recycling. All material that goes into the garden and on the plate makes its way back into the garden and onto the plate. It's a way of maintaining balance without extra resources like store-bought fertilizer. It's incredibly effective at reducing waste.

Those carrot tops you don't use in your stew—put them into the compost heap where they will break down and later feed future carrots you grow—but only after you clip off the greens and sprinkle on roasted veggies. Or you can make a pesto out of them. Carrot greens are edible and nutrient dense.

One more tangent here. You would be amazed at how many edible parts of the plants we throw away. Tamara's story taught us that sweet potato leaves are edible. I make a weekly sauté with their leaves, onions, garlic, and whatever else is growing in the garden. It's delicious.

It's important to do a little research before trying different parts of your plants. Some things will make you sick. For example, potato greens are not edible. One of my neighbors made a smoothie with them once. A minute before taking a sip, a friend called her. She boasted about her healthy shake. Her friend told her to pour it down the sink.

Potato greens are not edible. But sweet potato greens are because they are sweet and wouldn't dream of hurting anyone.

Let's go even further down the rabbit hole of closed-loop gardening.

NO PEEING ON THE GRASS.

The urine that you flush down the drain? That can be saved (I know. Ew!) and used as fertilizer for your plants. Please don't start making your kids run out and pee on your broccoli!

There's a method to the madness. There are helpful resources about using urine as fertilizer in your book bonus guide. Visit: www.createwellnessproject.com/bookbonus. You'll find them under the subcategory Poo and Pee for Happy Trees. Yes, I really do like using the word "poo."

There are homesteaders who use their toilet water (urine water only) to water their plants. This was a mind-blowing discovery for me. With help from a plumber, they divert their yellow toilet water into a small artificial stream.

The first section of the stream filters the water with a plant they don't eat. The naturally filtered water continues through the stream to water their crops on either side.

All this talk about drought, and we are literally flushing usable water down the drain.

Okay. Okay. I'm aware that this may be just too much for you at this moment. Are you making a stink face? Is your nose scrunched up in horror? Take a deep breath. It's going to be all right.

Before we get into the super scary stuff, like composting dog poo, let's take a step back.

There's another type of gray water that can be reused in the garden. The water that you use for washing clothes and dishes and your hands. Whew. Sweet relief that the lady is finally getting away from the smelly stuff. More is coming, though. Be prepared.

If you decide to divert your gray water into your garden, it's important to use non-harmful soaps in your household.

COMPOSTING DOG POO

Although Lucy's love of composting is unparalleled, Mitch started experimenting, too. Do you remember how much he abhors waste? Well, he got to thinking. Who creates a ton of waste in his family that he just bags up and throws in the trash every single day? His dog!

He searched how to compost dog feces and got a lot of conflicting information. Some videos warned that it was deadly for humans to use composted dog poo for gardens. Others suggested buying $400 compost containers for dog poo. For those contraptions, you add store-bought enzymes to break them down.

That made no sense to Mitch. In natural areas like forests, dogs poo everywhere. Without a $400 compost can and without a human adding enzymes to the poo, it breaks down fine on its own. And sometimes, a fruit tree uses the nutrients from the composted material as food.

Mitch didn't want to play Russian roulette with his family's health. So, he decided to learn more. It turns out that compost from dog feces is safer if you bury it under a tree that you plant. He knew that fresh dog feces would burn the roots. So, he created a separate compost container for his dog's poo.

There are different types of fertilizer that you can use on your homestead. Horse manure needs about six to nine months of composting to be ready for garden use. Chicken manure is ready in about nine months, but many gardeners wait twelve months before using it. Rabbit poo can be applied directly to your garden as it's considered cold. We talked a little bit about this in chapter seven.

Mitch compiled different recommendations on aging dog manure. He finally decided to take the longest time as his guideline. He ages it for twenty-four months. Mitch takes a page out of Lucy's book and doesn't turn it all that much. He is okay with waiting two years for it to cook if necessary.

It's important to note that their dog, Star, is not on any medication. She eats a whole food diet—no recalled kibble for that pooch. So, Mitch knows exactly what his dog manure is made of.

Mitch customized a large plastic tote. He drilled air holes in the bottom of the container and around the top border of the sides. He knew that flies would come if he left the poop exposed. Every few days, he picks up dog poo with a garden trowel. Then he lifts the lid and throws the poo into the container. (To save you from looking up the word "trowel," it's a small handheld garden shovel.)

After depositing the waste, he grabs a few handfuls of dry grass clippings and covers the deposit. It is amazing! No smell—no flies—no weird smelling disposable dog poo bags filling up his trash can.

Who invented those perfumed dog poo bags anyway? That must be the worst invention ever. I don't want to smell dog poo mixed with the offensively sweet smell of fake flower essences. No, thank you!

Nope. None of that for Mitch, either. Nothing but soon-to-be black gold.

As I write this, I'm reminding myself that I need to go out and scoop up my dog's poop from this week. It's the holiday season, and I've been remiss in cleaning up my dog's area this week. It's an easy ten-minute chore that will bring fantastic compost rewards.

Every few months, Mitch uses a watering can to moisten the compost. It took about seven months to fill up his first container. He didn't know what to do with it. So, he put it under his outdoor potting table. While it was cooking, he started looking for other gardeners who were composting poo.

He found a quirky, cool permaculturist named Brad Lancaster in Tucson, Arizona. Brad shared on YouTube how to safely and effectively compost human poo. That video is also listed in the Compost section of your book bonus guide: www.createwellnessproject.com/bookbonus.

From Brad's video, he learned about a tool that could help him turn the poo pile without touching it. Turning it didn't smell nearly as nice as the forest floor smell his daughter experiences. But it was the beginning of figuring out how to create something useful. And bonus! He kept something out of the landfill.

COFFEE GROUNDS

Mitch and Lucy decided to go one step further. They wanted to keep other people's trash out of landfills, too. Once a week, they visit their local diner for breakfast. They've known Carine, their waitress, for years now. Chatting with her has become another part of their community-building routine. They asked Carine if she would save the diner's coffee grounds for them. She was happy to see them turned into something other than trash.

After their meal, Mitch pulls the car up behind the diner. He gives the busboy an empty plastic tote and in turn, receives another tote filled with coffee grounds. He bought two totes to make it easy to transport the coffee grounds.

Most of the time, Lucy uses the coffee grounds in her compost pile. She occasionally sprinkles them on the garden beds to feed their resident worms. She doesn't put coffee grounds directly on plants or roots. Just a little confetti here and there.

VERMICOMPOSTING

Around the same time, Lucy decided to try her hand at vermicomposting. This is an amazing option for homesteaders who live in apartments, as it can be compact and discreet. One homesteader kept a vermicomposting container under her kitchen sink. Her husband didn't notice it for a whole year. Another vermicomposter keeps his bin at the bottom of his coat closet.

For those of us who are currently without a yard, it's easy to keep a vermicomposting bin. You can place it on your balcony, patio, cellar, or even carport.

My bin is on a potting table in the dog run. I often tease my husband by telling him that I need to empty my bin into the bathtub to warm everybody up. It freaks him out every single time.

What's so freaky about it? Well, I'm suggesting we fill our bathtub with worms. Yup, that's what vermicomposting is. It's a worm farm. Why is it such a great thing to have, though?

For a gardener, a worm farm is great when you want to take some of your crops and disperse them into areas of your garden. You're growing a worm crop to help your garden have better soil. You're also growing a worm crop to make compost faster. The worms will do the turning for you.

Lucy has a smaller worm farm made from a plastic tote. If a worm population outgrows a bin, it will equalize the population. This usually happens by the worms eating each other and having fewer offspring. So, she regularly grabs a handful of worms and relocates them from the bin into a garden bed.

Mitch put a handful of her worms in his dog poo bin. Both Lucy and Mitch were a little worried for those worms. Would they survive? Would they eat dog poo? It turns out they grew to be big and fat on dog poo and grassing clippings.

The key to getting compost worms to eat feces is to keep the feces separate from other types of food. If you feel bad for your poo worms and throw melon peels in the bin, they will ignore the poo.

OH, FOR THE LOVE OF WORMS!

Worms are amazing creatures. They breathe through their skin. They can regenerate certain parts of their bodies. They are hermaphrodites. They are so important that Charles Darwin's last book was dedicated solely to our muddy buddies.

David Attenborough has a video where he shows the largest Australian earthworm. It's nine feet long! I am a huge fan of worms and how they benefit our soil but a worm taller than a grown man? That's a bit much.

What exactly do worms do in the garden? Here's just the tip of the iceberg on what worms can do.

- They are natural recyclers. They eat waste like fallen fruit, animal scat, and dried leaves. Their waste then feeds the plants in that area.
- By making little tunnels to move around, they aerate the soil. Aerate means to bring air into something. Super compact dirt is too hard for plants to grow roots. Worms loosen up the soil, which makes it easier for plants to grow their roots deeper.
- They help with drainage. A no-till garden with an abundance of worms drains water better. This is also beneficial to plants because too much water can cause root rot.

If you need to know more, pick up Darwin's book and start a book club. That's certainly a weird enough book club for geeks like me to join!

EASY-BREEZY END OF CHAPTER TASKS

- Perhaps composting is not big on your list of projects you are interested in tackling. What is on your list? Use your journal now to write down every last homesteader mindset goal you have. This is a working list. So, don't belabor it. Add whatever comes to mind at this moment. Over the next couple of days, new ideas will come to you. Add those, too.

- Highlight the top three most exciting projects. On a new page, write the project name and then a few sentences about how to simplify the process. Go back and read chapter six if you feel like you're getting stuck in analysis paralysis.

- Take one of the three chosen projects in item two. Schedule a fifteen-minute appointment with yourself some time in the next seven days. Write the project name in the appointment slot. Spend that time doing one uncomplicated step. This step should be in the direction of completing this task. Your fifteen minutes might be spent writing out a task list of five-minute mini-steps. Or it could be searching online for "how to _____ the easy way."

PART FOUR

THE POCKET PUZZLE PLAN

One of the most effective ways to design a homesteader mindset is the Pocket Puzzle Plan. This is a life design that fits your reality. In this part of the book, we cover the plan. It is a step-by-step process to establish a fundamental basis for your homesteader mindset.

The name Pocket Puzzle Plan explains the homesteader mindset concept. It's a plan that fits in your pocket and works as gently as putting together a puzzle on a rainy vacation day. I've developed it from years of creating a homesteader mindset myself and witnessing others do the same.

THREE-STEP POCKET PUZZLE PLAN

Step One: Pick your corner.

Step Two: Immerse yourself during found time.

Step Three: Make your homesteader mindset a priority.

If you'd like to remember with an acronym, PIP works. Pick, Immerse, Priority. We'll discuss each step in the following three chapters. The word "pip" has two meanings. It can be used to describe a small seed. It also means an attractive thing. The PIP in your Pocket Puzzle Plan is certainly a small seed that will bring you attractive fruit.

There was always one big question in my mind concerning a homesteader mindset. How do certain people change their lives for the better without huge upheaval? This was followed up by a second important question. How can this seamless change be replicated?

For me, my homesteader mindset journey took off when I started learning French. I know that sounds strange. Learning a language has nothing to do with eating healthier and growing my own food. But dedicating time to something that exists solely to give me pleasure was a huge shift for me.

I have always been a dutiful girl. If it needs to be done, I will do it. If someone needs help, I try my best to step up. My husband's favorite question is "Are you doing this because you want to do it or because you think you have to do it?" That stops me in my tracks. I spent the first forty years of my life doing things I had to do. Even the fun things were a chore.

When I decided to learn French, I committed to doing it for amusement. For joy. For delight. Learning French was my first corner.

And French taught me a lot about myself. I learned things that helped me when I decided a few years later to start homesteading in the suburbs. It was an enlightening experience.

I realized that I love learning through reading. During the first two years of language learning, I read over thirty books in French. It was such fun for me to sit down and puzzle through a page or two each night.

When it was time to learn how to garden, I bought a number of paperback books to get me started.

I'm not a superfan of audio learning. Still, I immersed (step two) myself in language learning while I washed dishes each morning. *The Fluent Show* was my favorite language-learning podcast. The host, Kerstin Cable, is down-to-earth. Her methods are smart and approachable.

This was a habit that I transferred to permaculture when I delved into growing my own food.

After a few years, I started teaching people how to learn a language. I am a language coach and co-host of the *Language Hacking Podcast* with

Benny Lewis. Pleasure and work mingled as I learned more about healthy habit creation.

I took my habit building skills and moved them into my medicinal kitchen habits.

Looking back, I can see how my commitment to joy brought me life skills that I am now using in other projects. My personal bliss journey was an eye-opener. I never once writhed in anguish about my language-learning tasks. This was because I did and still do the things I thoroughly love doing. If something is difficult but necessary, I find a way to make it fun.

I also didn't need to stop all other parts of my life to learn French and now Spanish. I learned how to create routines. These routines afford me adequate time with the language while still living my life. This was step three.

If time management is a bear, you might want to add *The Bullet Journal Method* by Ryder Carroll to your reading list. It's an insightful look into the minds of well-organized people. I use this method to prioritize my days and get things done mindfully.

If we look back even a little further, this idea of balance comes from my graduate school studies. While training to become an acupuncturist and medical herbalist, I realized something. A healthy balance between school and life was essential. There was a slew of midterms and finals every eight weeks. Even so, my mental and emotional health was a priority.

We take the lessons we've had up to now with us each day. We can ignore our wisdom and tumble down the escalator. This leads to being taken up a few steps before tumbling again. Or we can use our knowledge, grab the handrail, and enjoy the ride.

You're reading this today because you want to enjoy the ride. You're interested in learning how.

These are steps people have followed to build a homesteader mindset. Some of us, like me, created these steps by happy accident. But many folks repeat these steps in new aspects of their lives.

We're going to dive into them right now.

CHAPTER 11:

STEP ONE—PICK YOUR CORNER

One of the more popular warnings that new homesteaders receive is "Don't bite off more than you can chew." Hold off on digging up your entire front lawn. Instead, spend a season or two growing food in a manageable area. This allows you time to learn the process while doing it without getting overwhelmed.

Did I heed this advice in my yard when I first started? Nope. My husband had to look at a patch of brown dirt for about a year before I finally did something with it. I started big by digging up every inedible plant in our front garden patch. Then I proceeded to procrastinate because I was overwhelmed. My success started when I went to the garden store and showed them a photo of my dirt. I asked them for plants that would not die easily.

The compassionate salesperson gave me four herbs that grow like weeds in my area. I planted them around the border of the brown patch, and that was my corner of the puzzle. It took me ten minutes to purchase them at the store and fifteen minutes to plant them.

For the next week or so, I was glowing with pride. The four herbs were a huge improvement from an empty dirt lot. Instead of feeling defeated or embarrassed every time I walked by, I felt empowered. It was a work in progress.

I took a burdensome project and breathed new life into it. And it took me less than a half hour. From there, adding three plants each week was easy. Now, we have a front garden full of edible plants. There are four different basil plants, oregano, rosemary, thyme, two types of tomatoes, five different pollinator flowers, two lemongrass bushes, and a few more. All from placing one puzzle piece at a time.

The first P in our helpful mnemonic, PIP, is for pick. Pick your corner.

How do you know what bite is too big to chew? You don't. The best way to figure it out is to start with an amount that seems almost too easy. You start in the corners of the puzzle and work your way out.

Imagine your Pocket Puzzle Plan as an actual puzzle. What are the pieces that most people look for first? Usually, the edges because there's less guesswork when you start to create the edge of the puzzle. And corners have two edges. Score!

Let's look at how Tamara used step one to learn a new skill. She picked one corner at a time. Then, she built out from her small successful corners. She wasn't focusing on the beautiful complete image of her puzzle. She just needed to start somewhere that would motivate her to keep going.

What was Tamara's new skill? Cooking.

Let's get one thing straight. Our friend, Tamara, detested cooking. She enjoyed tasty food but could rarely afford a restaurant meal. She opted for cheap, packaged food. The more she read up on the art of happiness, the more she realized that good health played a big part.

That was her first corner. She wanted to learn how to make a few nutritious, delicious, yet inexpensive meals at home. How on earth could she do that when she couldn't stand the thought of staring at a pot of water and waiting for it to boil?

She decided to dip her toe into this new habit very, very, very slowly. The first week, she committed to having one piece of fresh fruit per day. Wait a minute! That's not cooking. No, it's not. But it was the easiest piece of her puzzle plan she could find.

By the end of week one, she was inspired to sprinkle cinnamon on her apple slices. She didn't plan on adding spice to her one fruit a day goal, but it was easy and yummy. She bought a few tiny packets of different spices to see what she liked. Experimenting with new fruit and spice combinations was a game. Her taste buds relished new discoveries. Cardamon on her pears was surprisingly tasty.

Each evening, she would satisfy her curiosity by looking up the health benefits of her new snacks. This felt like a reward for her updated choices. It also gave her insight into how she could help her ailments with simple diet changes.

With the success of her fruity extravaganza, Tamara was encouraged to keep going. She decided that week two would focus on cooking protein that she could easily reheat. The easiest option seemed to be chicken breast.

After a little online searching for the easiest chicken recipes, she was ready for week two. She bought one pound of chicken breast. This would give her four servings. To make it super easy, she baked the chicken in her toaster oven with olive oil, salt, and pepper.

She ate her first serving for dinner that night with a side of canned green beans and her favorite pita bread. It wasn't exciting, but it was palatable. And yes, canned green beans are not something any nutritionist would recommend. But remember, she was focusing on the easy wins.

For lunch the next day, she made a chicken salad with a slice of toast. She used store-bought salad dressing to keep it simple. She liked this meal so much that she ate it again for lunch the next day.

For her last serving, she made a chicken sandwich. She didn't know what condiments to put on the sandwich. Thanks to DuckDuckGo, she chose tomato, lettuce, and mustard. It was her best creation yet!

You would have thought Tamara had won the lottery. She was elated to come home from work and have an uncomplicated meal in her fridge. The small addition of veggies helped her digestion. She also noticed that her energy was more stable. These physical changes gave her the incentive to keep going.

For week three, she decided to take a break. Her schedule was busy, and she was too tired to try something new. Tamara wanted this to be a lifestyle change. She knew that forcing herself to add something new each week could create burnout. That was not an option for her.

During week three, she continued to fill her mind each evening with books on happiness. One author talked a great deal about the art of letting go. What was she holding on to that needed to be let go? The biggest thing was her repeated self-talk about how much she hated cooking. Although she was making progress with her kitchen skills, every task came with a sigh.

Sigh. *I have to look up recipes. I hate doing this.*

Sigh. *Time to bake the chicken. What a drag.*

Sigh. *Cooking stinks!*

Taking a break from her cooking corner helped her reassess what was working and not working. Negative self-talk was not working. But how to change it? The first step was recognizing it. The second step was getting curious about it. Why did she hate cooking? Was it because it was something new? New things tended to cause Tamara stress.

She journaled a bit about this. Yes, new things stress her out a bit but nothing is new forever. The first time she made a cappuccino at work, she was super nervous. The second time was easy. And now, she makes an exceptional cappuccino with little thought. Cooking could be like that, too.

But how to bridge the gap? As she was journaling, Julie Andrews' voice popped into her head. She heard Julie belting out the song, "A Spoonful of Sugar." Aha! She would make her cooking sweet. No, she wouldn't douse her baked potato in maple syrup. She would make the experience sweet.

Her older sister had a unique idea. Once a month, she would make a special meal from a different country. She would play music from the country while she and her family were enjoying the meal. For example, she'd cook up a traditional German meal. Her children would take turns picking out German songs to play during dinnertime. They had such fun discussing what they thought about the food and the soundtrack.

What songs go with green beans? Although this idea was a bit advanced for Tamara at that moment, she did love listening to music. That was one way to add a little sweetness to her cooking experience. She would put on her favorite playlist just before washing her hands. It made her time in the kitchen special.

The next day she decided to add enjoyment to her cooking. She focused on emotionally nourishing food. She made a list in her journal of foods that gave her comfort. Here are a few examples to give you an idea.

Chicken Noodle Soup: Mom made it for me whenever I was sick. Even though it was canned soup, it felt like a warm bowl of love.

Tacos: My high school friend and I would watch reruns of our favorite TV show. We'd eat takeout tacos from our favorite Mexican restaurant. I wonder whether I could make them at home.

Roasted Potato and Broccoli: Uncle Mike used to make this for every family gathering. It was my favorite side dish. It reminds me of playing outside with my cousins.

From this list, she decided chicken noodle soup would be her next experiment. She chose a playlist and spent five minutes searching for the easiest recipe she could find. Since standing in front of a pot was not something she wanted to do on a regular basis, she invested in a slow cooker. She figured she could make a large batch of soup and freeze some for a healthier version of fast food. She found a Crock-Pot at the nearby thrift store and was ready to crock and roll. Yes, I am very proud of that play on words. Thank you for noticing.

Tamara built her corner from chicken breast and canned beans to a steamy chicken soup. She couldn't believe how good her soup was. It was the best chicken soup she'd ever had. And it came from her kitchen!

Tamara looked at this experience as a series of experiments. There was no disappointment when something went wrong. She either tweaked the recipe to better suit her taste, or she tossed the idea entirely. There was no ego attachment to how well she cooked or even how long it took her to learn how to cook. The reward was hidden in the act of learning something new. The bonus was warm food in her happy belly.

Pick your corner. That's where you will start your homesteader mindset project. Cooking. Community building. Growing herbs. Composting. Raising Livestock. Prioritizing Family time. Engaging in Permaculture. Homesteading. The choice is up to you.

Commit to five minutes per day. Maybe the first five minutes is writing down answers to the questions at the end of this chapter. Maybe you ask your friend or spouse to brainstorm with you. Perhaps you read an article about your corner. There is a myriad of possibilities for how to start. The key is that you actually do something for five minutes.

As you achieve small success, branch out into different corners. Tamara became interested in growing food before she started cooking. The successful growing of basil inspired her to start adding it to her meals. Once you have a month of tiny yet steady successes, allow yourself to add more pieces to the puzzle. Maybe five minutes a day grows to twenty minutes three times a week.

Use play as the guiding principle. When you hit a stumbling block (which will happen!), ask yourself how you can make this activity fun. What will help sweeten the pot?

Allow curiosity to run wild. Ask more questions. Find answers to them. Be childlike in your wonder. How many hearts do worms have? Is hibiscus edible? What's the easiest way to raise hens for eggs?

Need some ideas on how to get started? Here are a few.

Cooking: Learn how to bake a whole chicken. You have no idea how many times I've heard the question "What should I do first in homesteading?" The experts often suggest learning to bake a whole chicken. Why? Because it's surprisingly easy to do and it's versatile. You can make countless dishes from leftover chicken.

We are working our way through a half chicken this week. We started with chicken and potatoes—moved onto chicken wrapped in ham with melted cheese—added chili peppers and sautéed yellow peppers for a spicy flare. The possibilities are endless.

And when you are ready for a challenge, save the chicken bones to make chicken broth. After I've used the chicken carcass for broth, I bury it about two feet under a new tree or bush that I'm ready to plant. It's a simple way to compost meat by-products.

I learned how to make chicken broth from the sweetest lady on the internet. Her name is Mary. Her YouTube channel is *Mary's Nest*. She's got this gentle way of explaining things that immediately chills me out.

Community Building: If you're a natural hostess, plan a park party around an activity that interests you. I've offered free Qigong in the park and met a lovely group of people. My husband has hosted a few tea tastings.

We invite friends and post invitations on social sites. This is a great way to meet like-minded people.

If planning an event is not your thing, search for community events using your area. For example, I typed "composting" and my city into a search engine. I found a few non-profit organizations with free events. You could attend an event and even consider volunteering.

Growing Herbs: Herbs truly are the easy start to growing a garden. They are often quite hardy. So, beginners will get immediate success seeing at least one of them do well. They are great for learning how to keep a plant alive. If you're overwatering, the plant will tell you by getting sick or even dying. This is not a bad thing. Well, it's bad for the plant.

For you, it's a learning experience. Take a pic of your sad plant and show it to your nearby garden center. They will help you troubleshoot it. If you don't feel like trudging out to the store, you can describe the problem online. Look for images that match your problem. Once you know the problem, you can search for solutions.

Composting: This is one of my favorite corners for starting. You have no idea how rewarding it is to take waste and turn it into fertile soil. It's relatively easy, too. I could write a book solely on composting because I adore the process. But there's already a great book out there. I recommended it earlier, but it's important enough to mention it again. It's *Compost Everything* by David The Good.

Raising Livestock: Stop shaking your head already. Livestock doesn't have to be complicated. The essential ingredient to keeping it simple is to start small. Maybe you want to learn how to raise meat rabbits as healthy dog food for your puppy.

One way to start small is to adopt a rabbit from your local animal shelter. This rabbit will live a long, luxurious life as you have no idea where that poor thing has been. And it would be creepy to adopt animals to eat. Just sayin'.

The adopted rabbit will teach you how to raise a rabbit. If you want to create a closed loop, you can also grow your rabbit's food. The adopted rabbit won't be a freeloader. He contributes as your rabbit raising mentor and homegrown cold fertilizer factory. The two benefits of your adopted rabbit are also called stacking functions.

Once you know how to care for a rabbit, you could build a rabbitry and buy three meat rabbits to start your livestock. Springing your first rabbit out of the slammer while learning the art of rabbit rearing is a win-win. A win for you. A win for the adopted rabbit. A win for the overwhelmed animal shelter.

Prioritizing Family Time: What is a homesteader mindset without your family? If you don't have a traditional family, that's okay. You can call any of the people you love family. The important thing is that you make family time a priority.

This corner can start with something as simple as calling your mom once a week on your commute home. It could also be a game night every week. Connection comes in all forms. To create trust and deepen relationships, you need time. Make that time, and your family will start to bloom.

Engaging in Permaculture: This is another topic I cannot stop talking about. Permaculture is a method of designing your landscape to mimic nature. Lots of people who use permaculture create food forests. This is a combination of perennial and annual plants that live close to each other in guilds. Each plant offers one or more benefits to its neighboring plants as well as the gardener.

Are you familiar with the words perennial and annual? Generally speaking, a perennial plant is one that grows year after year. An apple tree is a perennial. An annual plant is one that grows for a season, creates seeds, and dies. Watermelon is an example of an annual.

I had a hard time remembering this at first. I started telling myself, "I plant annuals annually." That seemed to do the trick for keeping them straight.

One way to start with the corner of permaculture is to watch any of Geoff Lawton's videos. He gives a lot of property tours, which will give you ideas on where to start. I've created an extensive list of permaculture materials for you. I categorized the list into books, podcasts, and YouTube channels. That list is a great place to get started. Visit: www.createwellnessproject. com/bookbonus. You'll find them in the Permaculture section.

Homesteading: Like Mitch and Lucy, I didn't know there was a proper name for what I was doing. Homesteading is a lifestyle of self-sufficiency. It's a fluid term that has many meanings to many people. Hard-core homesteaders might define it as living 100 percent off the grid. Suburban homesteaders like me might define it as creating closed-loop systems. A beginner homesteader might start as small as using glass jars rather than plastic.

I've created another list of homesteading resources to help you get started. You can access them at the same book bonus link just mentioned. They are in the Homesteading section.

EASY-BREEZY END OF CHAPTER TASKS

- Pick your corner. When you sit down and imagine how wonderful a homesteader mindset will be, what stands out?

  - Take a timer and set it for five minutes. Allow yourself to daydream about your ideal homesteader mindset. After the timer goes off, write down a list of five to ten things that gave you pleasure during the daydream. Hint: You can use the list you made in chapter ten to inspire you.

- Choose one of the items on your list as your starting puzzle piece. Pick the one that seems the most fun or the easiest. Are you having trouble deciding? Is the indecision causing procrastination? If yes, pick the third one on your list.

  - Take a piece of paper and write down your corner. This is the beginning of your Pocket Puzzle Plan. Leave space at the bottom of the paper and on the opposite side of the paper. You will create a few more important lists later in this book.

  - Your corner statement should be clear, decisive, and positive. Here are three examples.

    - I am learning how to grow my own food. It's rewarding.

    - I am making family connection time. This is important to me.

    - I am studying traditional cooking. Eating well is essential.

  - Your puzzle plan should be able to fit into your wallet easily. If you want to use a letter size paper, that's fine as long as it fits comfortably into your wallet or cell phone case. I like to use an index card folded in half as it's sturdy for taking in and out of my wallet.

- Once you have your starting puzzle piece, commit to making contact with it once a day for five minutes. Let me repeat that for emphasis. Your goal is five minutes a day.

○ If you reach five minutes and want to do more, that's great. However, you are a success every time you make contact with the puzzle piece for a mere five minutes.

○ For now, five minutes a day could be spent reading a book about the topic. As you read it, you'll get ideas on what your next right action is. Write those ideas in your Homesteader Mindset Journal or on the front page of this book.

○ How do you commit to this goal?

  ▪ Write it down.

  ▪ Tell someone you trust about it and ask them whether you can text, email, or call them every day when you've completed the goal. You can do this in an online community setting where others are sharing their goals. Or you can pick one friend and use them as your accountability partner.

CHAPTER 12

STEP TWO—IMMERSE YOURSELF DURING FOUND TIME

In chapter eleven, I invited you to make a five-minute daily commitment to your first puzzle piece. Five minutes is a useful starting goal. It's small enough to do even when you're tired but big enough to keep the task in the forefront of your mind. As you move forward, you'll start adding time to your daily commitment.

Add time? Am I silly for suggesting that? Perhaps you don't even have five minutes to spare. How in tarnation are you going to do anything consistently with no free time? Hold your horses, Yosemite Sam. I've got a few tools to help.

This chapter will show you how to use the I in your PIP. Immerse yourself in found time.

We'll go through each one individually, starting with my favorite.

HABIT STACKING

Pick a concrete habit and stack another onto it. Examples of concrete habits in your life include brushing your teeth and eating.

I first read about this concept in the outstanding book *Atomic Habits* by James Clear. Once I started implementing it in my life, it was amazing how much I could accomplish.

Lindsay Williams of *LindsayDoesLanguages.com* breaks this down into two subcategories: habit piles and habit chains. Many of those with a homesteader mindset do both several times a day. Let's take a look at Jim's habit stacking.

Habit Pile: A habit pile is where you add a new habit to an existing habit that happens at the same time. Earlier, Jim showed us a stellar example of a habit pile. He used his morning commute to check in with the real estate agent who was helping him find a smaller home.

If you have a commute, you can make excellent use of the time in the car. Once a week, download a few informative podcasts about your current puzzle piece. Listen to them in the car. I usually download ten or so in case a few of them are duds.

Habit Chain: A habit chain is where you add a new habit by linking it to an existing habit. Once again, Jim modeled this. Once he cut his commute time down to ten minutes, he had fifty minutes extra in his afternoon. He linked the end of his workday with visits to the coffeehouse to work on his current puzzle piece. Brainstorming at the coffeehouse was linked with the established habit of leaving the office. This made it easier to implement.

FOUND TIME

Found time can appear in several surprising ways. The key is to be on the lookout for it. A few habit experts sometimes call it dead time, but that's too morbid for me.

In Jim's case, a change in his routine offered him fifty minutes of found time every morning and afternoon. If he hadn't been actively looking to capitalize on found time, he could have easily wasted that time. How often do we piddle away time reading the news in the morning and playing video games in the afternoon?

A lot of times, we don't even realize how much time gets eaten up by TV, news, social media, and video games. Don't get me wrong. There is a time and place for passive entertainment. However, Americans tend to spend hours in front of a screen with very little time left for actual living. One of my favorite books on the topic is *Digital Minimalism* by Cal Newport. He offers multiple easy solutions.

Many employees of social media companies do not have social media accounts themselves. I know! I was shocked, too. A fascinating book about the problems of social media is *Ten Arguments for Deleting Your Social Media Accounts Right Now* by Jaron Lanier.

I digress. Let's get back to the concept of found time. This can be anytime you find yourself pulling out your cell phone to kill time—in the doctor's office waiting room—while watching *Frozen* with your five-year-old for the 873rd time—during a boring work meeting via Zoom. (Come on! I know you've done that.)

By putting a few tools on your phone, you can use that established habit of filling up found time. Add an audiobook about your current project to your phone. Download a digital book that you can read for five minutes at a time. This would count toward the five-minute commitment that you made in chapter eleven.

As much as I detest social media, there is a way to use it for good, not evil. In moderation, of course. Consider creating an account that is solely for the purpose of your homesteader mindset. Don't add your friends, relatives, or celebrities. Add accounts that have what you want.

Sara created a traditional cooking account on Instagram. On it, she shared pictures of her first attempts at meal batching. She found hashtags that connected her to a traditional cooking community.

I did the same with learning French. I wrote an article that spells out my how-to. The link to it is available in your free book bonus guide. You can take many of those tips and translate them (pun intended) for your current puzzle piece.

OPTIMAL TIME OF DAY

Figuring out the best time of day for working on your puzzle plan is of utmost importance. Jim learned this the hard way. He always admired

Sara's early bird routines. She often had hours of tasks completed before Jim rolled out of bed.

When he started working on downsizing their family home, he tried waking up an hour earlier. It worked for two days. And those two days were a struggle. He felt groggy and grumpy. He liked the idea of being an early bird, but his night owl reality did not approve.

He started taking notice of when he was more creative. He realized that he got a burst of energy around 10 p.m. From 10 p.m. to 11 p.m., he found himself looking at videos of projects that fascinated him.

For a few months, it was pioneer cooking. There was a fella who would show his YouTube audience how to cook recipes from early America. Jim loved these videos. They gave him ideas on how to incorporate interesting ingredients into his cooking. It also provided historical tidbits he could discuss with his son, Zach, who loved cooking.

One night while watching a pioneer cooking show, a lightbulb went off. What if he dedicated fifteen minutes each evening to one of his puzzle pieces? He could be done by 10:15 p.m. and enjoy the rest of his second wind doing whatever tickled his fancy.

This idea was a huge success for Jim. He found himself often using up his entire hour of energy on pieces of his current project. It gave him great pleasure to talk about his discoveries over breakfast the next morning.

Sara, a natural early bird, continued working on her projects in the morning before the rest of the house woke up. At both times, the house was quiet, and they enjoyed a peaceful time of extended focus.

What about you? What time of day are you most productive? It doesn't just have to be morning or evening. Maybe lunchtime is when you find yourself creatively inspired. We explore this more in the end of the chapter review.

ACCOUNTABILITY PARTNER

This is where the rubber meets the road for me. When I have an accountability partner for my long-term projects, my consistency doubles. Humans are social beings. We do better when we're sharing and growing and building with others. Yes, even introverts like me.

Here are a few ways to find and utilize the power of an accountability partner.

The Friends & Family Plan: Pick a member. Any member. Say the previous two lines with a 1940s Atlantic City casino dealer accent.

But really, any member of your family or friend circle will do. As long as they are supportive of your goal, they are a good fit.

We saw Sara do this as she was learning how to cook for the first time in her life. She didn't learn how to cook until her late thirties. She thought it was a terrible waste of time. During her recovery, cooking became a priority. It is important for her to know what she is putting into their bodies.

Her energy and budget were limited. So, she decided to ask a few friends to teach her how to cook their favorite easy meal. All she needed to do was think about which friends served her the most delectable meals and call them up. They were delighted to help. Most foodies love to bring others into the club of cuisine.

These cooking events offered two benefits. As we would say in permaculture, Sara was stacking functions with these meetings. She was learning to cook, but she was also deepening her community ties. While they were cooking, Sara would offer an ear to a friend who was going through a rough time or vice versa. It became a healing gathering.

Sara also became an accountability partner for her child. Each week, Matthew's chore was to chop veggies for the family. This could be a daunting task for a young boy. So, Sara joined him in the task. She realized that giving him a chore without teaching him how to do it would be cruel.

Instead of leaving him to do it alone, Sara would help him get started during the first ten minutes. Then she would stay in the kitchen and complete another task while he finished up his chore. In this way, she was able to get a meal prepped while Matthew chopped. She was available for questions, but she let Matthew decide the details of his task. He was in charge of how he would cut the veggies and store them in the fridge.

This was another stacking of functions. Sara taught her child important lessons with this task. He learned about healthy food planning and finishing a task. It was a cherished time for Sara and her boy. They would often chat about what was important to him that day. They were able to bond during a household chore. How cool is that?

The best part for Matthew? The ritual of rooibos chai tea with honey that he and his mom enjoyed once that task was finished. We'll talk more about the beauty of rewards in a bit.

Local Events: Finding groups through local events is one way to build community. It's how Sara met her favorite walking companions. As part of her recovery plan, Sara wanted to start walking with the boys on a regular basis. She was having trouble making it a priority, though.

She found a slow hike group on Meetup and decided to give it a try. Sara and her sons started walking with this group weekly to help her create a routine. She became friends with another member of the group who also had two children. They decided to add an additional slow hike to their weekly schedule and offered to host it for the group.

Nextdoor is another website where you can find or post gatherings. It's a great way to meet more people who have similar interests. I once posted a French discussion group in my neighborhood. It was such fun to meet neighbors who loved learning French as much as I do.

Be forewarned. Nextdoor is a version of social media. You can waste a lot of time scrolling. Whenever I use sites like this, I turn off all notifications. That keeps me from getting sucked into the scroll of gloom.

Organizations: Organizations that cater to your interests are another way to find accountability. *The Power of Habit* by Charles Duhigg talks about the effectiveness of 12-Step groups. He mentioned Alcoholics Anonymous (AA). In AA, people replace their old habits with new ones—habits that include self-awareness, resilience tools, and social connection.

Jim used an organization to take cooking classes with his son. He searched "cooking classes near me" and read the reviews for the two companies closest to his home. Jim and his son enjoyed the cooking class so much that it grew into a regular event for them.

In the case of Jim's cooking class, the teacher was his accountability partner for that evening.

Online Communities: There are countless communities available to act as your accountability partners. Paid and free online groups are available for just about everything.

My first experience with this was working as a coach in the Fluent in 3 Months Bootcamp. Students pay a fee and enter the Fluent in 3 Months online universe. They are paired up with study buddies and coaches, and are guided on their journey to learning a new language.

Jim and his youngest son, Matthew, joined a Facebook group led by his son's favorite DIY builder. The Facebook group focused on building cool stuff with reusable materials. Each week, Matthew would share a photo of the progress he was making on his project. Jim had parental controls on Matthew's Facebook to be sure it was a safe place for his son to share.

In Matthew's case, the group worked as his accountability partner. He received the dopamine hit from seeing supportive comments on his photos. Members would also ask questions about his timeline goal and what his next project would be. This interaction infused Matthew with motivation to continue.

In Real Life (IRL) and Online Partners: Be on the lookout for accountability partners in your life. It's a wonderful way to develop a friendship with a current acquaintance.

We read about Jim doing this with a fellow church member. He and Brian both wanted to build chicken coops. So, they met at Jim's favorite coffeehouse on Tuesday afternoons to develop a plan. This is a perfect example of an IRL accountability partner.

Online partners are great for people who might not be well enough to leave their homes. It's also great for people with tricky schedules. While regaining her strength, Sara joined a homesteading community online. She posted a request for an accountability partner without success. As she got to know the other members of the group, she reached out via direct message to three women she admired. One of them agreed to be her accountability partner.

It's important to remember that not every action results in an immediate win. Do what Sara did. Keep trying new things to get the outcome you desire.

If you need a quick fix, the website Focusmate.com might be valuable to you. With Focusmate, you schedule time on their website. An accountability partner is assigned to you for the hour session. In the first minute, you and your accountability partner discuss what your plans are. Then you both get to work while staying online together. It's surprisingly effective. I used it to edit my first book.

Paid Coaches: Sara and Jim didn't have the budget for a paid coach. But Brian, Jim's chicken coop partner, invested in monthly coaching sessions to help organize his life. The accountability and group coaching calls were extremely helpful in getting him started.

BEING PHYSICALLY COMFORTABLE

This one seems so logical that you might not need to read about it, but I sure did. Kerstin Cable of *The Fluent Show* was the first person I heard mention this. I listened to her podcast non-stop when I was first learning languages. Her show was my chop-veggies-easy-listening go-to.

In one episode, she reminded us to make sure we are physically comfortable before starting a task. Her questions were along the lines of this:

Are you warm enough? Not too hot? Are you sitting in a comfy chair? Is the ambient sound conducive to concentration? Are you hungry? Do you have a glass of water close at hand?

I liken it to proper self-parenting. Recently, I spent some time at my beloved niece's home. She and her husband are raising an adorable two-year-old daughter. When they dress her up to ride in the car, they make sure she's eaten. They check to make sure her clothes are warm enough for the weather that day. Sometimes, they bring a beverage for her to sip on to make sure she's hydrated.

Good parents do this for their children. Why shouldn't we do this for ourselves?

CUE -> ROUTINE -> REWARD

I've mentioned *The Power of Habit* because it is one of my favorite books based on creating healthy habits. In the book, Charles explains the cue-routine-reward behavior loop: "This is how new habits are created: by putting together a cue, a routine, and a reward, and then cultivating a craving that drives the loop."

A cue is something that happens every day. It can trigger your brain to initiate the routine. A routine is an action you take that is the main part of the habit. A reward is what happens at the end of the routine to keep your brain craving the habit again.

Let's use Sara as an example. She has a healthy exercise routine. Most mornings, she walks her dog for twenty minutes. Here's a breakdown of that habit.

Cue: Her workout clothes are next to her bed. When she wakes up, she puts them on.

Routine: After brushing her teeth, she heads to where her furry accountability partner is patiently waiting. She grabs his leash, puts on her shoes, and out for a walk they go.

Reward: Besides a great deal of satisfaction in taking care of her dog, Sara rewards herself after the walk. She sips a nourishing cup of herbal infusion while gazing out the window at her garden. Satisfaction mixed with endorphins and a tasty beverage offer her the reward she craves.

Another secret that Sara used while creating this routine was timing. She started with a five-minute walk. That's right. Her pup only got a five-minute walk for the first week or so. This was how she established the most difficult part of the routine—getting started.

Once out of the house, she was often able to lengthen the walk to ten minutes. From there, she continued to grow the length of the walk as the habit became more established.

EASY-BREEZY END OF CHAPTER TASKS

- In what way can you habit stack to create more time for your puzzle pieces? Take out your journal, friend. It's time to brainstorm. Please write three potential habit piles and three possible habit chains.

    ○ Pick one to incorporate into your daily life this week.

    ○ If you're having trouble deciding which one, pick the easiest one. If you still can't decide, pick the second one on your list.

    ○ This habit stack counts as part of your five-minute daily commitment.

    ○ For extra credit, let your accountability partner know your progress daily. I did this every day while writing this book. I texted my writer friend with the amount of time I wrote. She did the same.

    ○ Let's give you a few examples to get your creative motor running. One of my habit piles happens while I drive to the farmers' market. During the drive, I listen to an audiobook on medicinal herbs. And here are two of my habit chains. Chop vegetables for five minutes after washing breakfast dishes. Prune my garden for seven minutes after watering the container garden.

- What time of day are you most productive? That's the time to incorporate your first habit stack.

    ○ If you're not sure, use this week to notice your energy. It might help to set an alarm on your phone every two hours and log what your energy is now on a scale of one to ten.

    ○ Ask your close friends and family when they notice you have the most energy.

- Create three cue-routine-reward cycles from your list of six habit stacks. Pull out your Pocket Puzzle Plan. Write three of these habit stacks under your corner statement.

    ○ Cue: Keep it simple.

- If you want to read a book as a habit, start by putting the book out where it's easy to access.

○ Routine: Keep it simple.

- Do what Sara did. Start super small and build on your success. If you want to read a chapter per day, start with one page per day and add pages until you're a reading champ.

○ Reward: Keep it simple. (Seeing a pattern yet?)

- Make your reward uncomplicated but something that brings you pleasure. Walking barefoot in the grass is a huge reward for me. One minute of grass between toes is an excellent payoff.

CHAPTER 13

STEP THREE—MAKE YOUR HOMESTEADER MINDSET A PRIORITY

In step one, you picked a corner to start the puzzle of your homesteader mindset. If you've experimented with step two, you've made time for your Pocket Puzzle Plan through immersion. The third and last step in your Pocket Puzzle Plan is quite important. Make your homesteader mindset a priority. This is the last P in PIP.

If you're reading through this book without doing any of the work, that's fine. I do recommend getting started sooner rather than later. Even peeking back at the previous chapters and writing out the answers to those questions will get you on your way. If you must read through to the end, have at it. The only thing I suggest is you start again reading and answering questions in chapter one. Do this before you put the book down, telling yourself you'll come back to it.

Back to step three, how does one make their homesteader mindset a priority?

This is a tricky question, isn't it? People pay a lot of lip service to what they call their priorities, while their actions don't back it up. Whenever I hear someone say, "I would do anything for my [insert person or pet here]," I look at their actions. Do they follow their words?

At times, a person's actions do not follow their words. These folks are not bad or unworthy. They are simply not naming their true priorities. If people were more honest, they might say, "My priority on weeknights is to numb out with snack food in front of the TV."

The way to shift priorities is to take contrary action. "I would rather numb out with pretzels and beer in front of the TV, but I committed to five minutes of reading. So, I'll do that first. Get it out of the way and then relax."

Trust me. This works. The fulfillment that you are lacking will begin to blossom. You won't need to anesthetize yourself any longer. You will find yourself looking forward to your Pocket Puzzle Plan.

Start small and build on your successes.

Let's take a look at Lucy's priority shift.

You might remember that famous '70s commercial. It featured a Native American looking at litter strewn at his feet. A single tear rolls down his cheek. He is grieving what has happened to his land.

Like many, this commercial affected Lucy. Her young daughter was haunted by the thought that her existence creates pollution. Such a big problem for such a tiny human. Both Lucy and her daughter are staunch anti-litter people.

Interesting to note that a soda company funded this ad. We all know large corporations are a huge part of the pollution problem. As many giant businesses go unchecked, individuals bear the burden of pollution guilt. This is an ongoing problem that leaves many feeling hopeless about the situation.

Mitch and Lucy were chatting one day. She was not sure how to shake this feeling of overwhelm. Environmental news was bleak. The more she read about the damage being done to the earth, the more paralyzed she became with worry. How could one person make a difference for the planet? What would be left for her children? Her grandchildren?

Her husband listened quietly and took a slow deep breath. "I've felt that way. Some days, it just feels like too much. What helps me is the reminder that action is the antidote to anxiety."

A lightbulb went off in Lucy's brain. What if she could make action a priority in her life? What if she could take one small action at a time to help her heal the earth and heal her mind?

Later that week, she read an interesting quote by Alice Walker: "Activism is my rent for living on the planet." What if she started paying her rent in small ways? How could she start with something easy to get her motivated to move out of fear and into action?

She was nursing this thought while watching her grandchild play on the swings. They often visited the playground near her daughter's house. It was a great way for the little ones to burn off energy. She reveled in watching them play with imagination. Making a sliding board an escape route from the dragon chasing them—or swinging into space.

She considered using her imagination to help her. What would a small but doable action look like? Her gaze rested on a nearby tree. A squirrel ran down at lightning speed. And there it was—her inspiration for change.

A small plastic straw lay at the bottom of the tree. She walked over, picked it up, and put it in the trash can. The rent had been paid.

Each time she visited the playground, she would pick up at least one piece of litter. Her husband bought her a cheap contraption for picking up litter without bending. She keeps her plastic arm extension in the car.

The action of picking up litter is marvelously effective for her anxiety. Whenever her mind starts to worry, she reminds herself that she is in the solution. Her brain has no space for worry.

At times, simple self-talk is enough. Other times, she needs more support. She keeps a list of tools in her wallet. She pulls out this list and works her way down them until the feeling of heaviness is lifted.

Sometimes she goes through the list twice before relief hits. A few times, she gets tired and needs a nap. But a nap is way more acceptable to her than anxiety.

What was on Lucy's list? Let's explore it together.

Literature: Lucy has two books that give her proper attitude alignments. One is a book of prayers. The other is a daily reader that expands on inspirational quotes. It covers topics like hope, courage, and peace.

Lucy reads one page from one of her books every morning. She keeps a small inspirational pamphlet in her purse for reading on the go. If she feels a little shaky emotionally, she'll whip out one of her books and read a page.

Sometimes, this is all she needs to feel like she is not alone. Oftentimes, she will open a book at random, and the page will be exactly what she needs.

Writing: Lucy learned long ago that writing creates space for her emotions. Her sponsor (mentor in Al-Anon) recommends that she write three lists every day.

Three things that she was grateful for,

Three things that she achieved that day,

And three things that she surrendered to a higher power.

This list usually takes her less than two minutes to create. Yet it helps her stay connected and redirect her internal dialogue.

When she feels anxious about an upcoming event, she writes. Sometimes, she describes the future scenario in the most positive light. She writes it out as if it already happened and it went swimmingly. This is another way to realign her thoughts.

Telephone: Lucy never understood the idea behind people talking about their troubles. It seemed like a big waste of time. Then she read a story about a hiker who saved himself from plunging into a frozen lake. It helped her understand the power of sharing.

The hiker was walking over a frozen lake when the ice beneath his feet started to crack. He knew that if he continued standing, he would create a hole in the ice and fall into freezing water. The ice could not support all of his weight in the concentrated area where his two feet were located.

He immediately laid down on the ice, creating what looked like an X with his body. This dispersed his weight on the ice. He then slithered to a safer area.

Lucy doesn't like talking about her feelings. But she knows that sharing them with another person will help ease the weight. She knows that if she holds it all in, she risks the chance of falling into a freezing lake of repressed emotions.

She has a circle of trusted friends from her weekly Al-Anon meetings. Calling other members to share about what's happening in their lives is recommended. Lucy tries to call at least two people per week. Even when she is busy, she will call one friend and one newcomer.

If she reaches her friend's voicemail, she has a formula for leaving a message.

Firstly, she talks about the problem. What happened to her, or what annoying thing someone said or did.

Secondly, she shares her part in the situation. Is she harboring resentment? Is she ruminating about the event? Is her ego tied up in this troubling situation? Is there a healthy boundary she hasn't created yet?

Thirdly, she commits to the next right action. A lot of times, the next action is one of the other items on her list of tools. She might commit to writing for five minutes about her feelings. Or she might say the Serenity Prayer. Other times, she reads a page from her literature. She might even call another friend and chat for a bit.

The secret here is that she always returns to what her part is and what her next right action will be.

As her years in Al-Anon grew, her friend circle deepened. There were three friends whom she felt she could tell anything. She kept them on speed dial on her cell phone.

She also coded her Al-Anon telephone numbers in her phone by putting AL in front of each of their contact names. This way, she could pick up the phone, search for AL friends, and make an outreach call with little planning.

The telephone is not only available to 12-Step members. You can develop these types of connections with friends you already have. It doesn't even need to be a formal request. Start by calling a friend that you know is having a tough week and checking in on them.

Service: Lucy didn't think she had many skills worth sharing, but she was dead wrong. She was perfectly capable of undertaking service positions at her weekly meetings. First, she helped make the coffee. Then, she was the timer.

The more she served, the more connected she felt to her community. When she helped the secretary of the meeting set up, she got to know her better. The result of service was a strong feeling of belonging in the group.

You don't have to be part of a 12-Step program to be of service. Service positions exist everywhere. You could volunteer as a receptionist at your yoga studio once a week. You could be a greeter at your place of worship. You could assist in your child's class every month. Wherever you normally frequent, there are opportunities to help.

Meditation: People often lump prayer and meditation into one item. They are two separate activities. Meditation is the art of listening. Praying is the art of speaking.

Meditation is something that people of all faiths and even atheists can do. The mental health benefits are numerous. One of my favorite books on the subject is *Buddha's Brain* by Rick Hanson.

In the book, he talks extensively about the life-changing effects of meditation. Rick writes, "To become happier, wiser, and more loving, sometimes you have to swim against ancient currents within your nervous system." Meditation helps retrain your nervous system by bringing awareness to your knee-jerk reactions. You learn to listen to your body's response rather than be ruled by it.

Lucy had never even considered meditation before her sponsor suggested it. The idea of it sounded both impossible and boring. How on earth could she sit still for hours? Who has time for that?

When her sponsor suggested she set a kitchen timer for one minute, she didn't see the point of it. But her sponsor suggested a lot of things that worked out for the better. So, she thought she'd give it a try.

Every morning before breakfast, she sat in a quiet corner of the bedroom. She moved the laundry basket off the unused chair, lit a candle, and closed her eyes. She committed to trying this form of meditation for thirty days.

She managed to sit quietly for twenty-eight of those days. It wasn't a perfect score, but it was a great start. This exercise didn't give her any feelings of peace during the sessions. It did, however, show her that she could sit every day in silence.

The next month, she committed to another thirty days. This time, she upped the time to five minutes per session. A friend who had been meditating for some time suggested she try guided meditations.

It was easy to swap out a five-minute silent meditation with a ten-minute guided meditation. In this way, she built a meditation practice that suited her needs.

Eventually, her daily practice included twenty minutes of silent meditation. Sometimes, she adds a guided meditation for sleep before bed.

After about three months, Lucy noticed that her anxious reactions had decreased by 50 percent. News that would have sent her into a worry spiral doesn't affect her the same anymore. Meditation is key for her peace of mind.

I've compiled a list of guided meditations that you might like to try. You can access this list at www.createwellnessproject.com/bookbonus. They are listed under Meditation.

Prayer: If meditation is listening and prayer is speaking, who are you speaking to? Well, that depends. If you have a faith practice, like Lucy, you will pray to your higher power. If you are an atheist or agnostic, you can pray to your higher self.

And yes, everyone has a higher self. Think about the times when you refrained from doing something ridiculous. That was thanks to your higher self.

Anne Lamott, the author of *Bird By Bird*, wrote, "Here are the two best prayers I know: 'Help me, help me, help me,' and 'Thank you, thank you, thank you.'"

I could end this section with that—thank you and help me—that's all you need. But let's go a little deeper.

How does regular prayer work? Let's take a quick look at how Lucy brought prayer into her routine.

Lucy started her prayer practice earlier in life. In her thirties, she had a forty-five-minute commute to work. One day, she was driving home with nothing interesting playing on the car radio. She shut it off.

Her first thought in the quiet hum of the automobile was "What now? How can I make use of this time?" A white shirt hanging out to dry flashed in her mind. She remembered back to her grandmother's prayer routine. Her grandmother would pray while hanging clothes on the line. Perhaps Lucy could pray until she reached her driveway.

That first prayer was awkward. She didn't know what to say. She decided to thank God for her blessings. As she began to list them, she felt lighter. The more she noticed her blessings, the more blessings came to the surface.

Her prayer routine was simple. Once she turned right at the T in the road, she would pray until she reached her driveway. That gave her about fifteen minutes for her conversation with her higher power.

She speaks out loud and informally as if God were sitting in the passenger seat next to her. The discussions are quite intense at times. When her oldest son moved away, she banged her fist on the steering wheel and insisted God protect him.

This regular routine of praying while driving continued after she retired. Only then, she needed to add more prayer time as she wasn't driving daily. Some days, she would take a walk on her country road and ask God to come with her.

Through these daily talks, her faith grew. Her connection to God and to her higher self deepened. Her prayers were never dressy. They were sturdy.

Mentorship: Simply put, a mentor is anyone who knows more about a subject than you and is available to guide you in your learning. I found a mentor when I first opened my acupuncture clinic. She became one of my closest friends in the process.

You don't need to go through an organization to find a mentor. Although, that's a valid possibility. All you need to do is find someone who has what you want and ask them if you could learn from them.

Lucy's personal development mentor was her sponsor in Al-Anon. She grew through the 12-Step program by attending meetings and working the steps. Her sponsor showed her how.

Is there someone in your life who has what you want? Maybe it's a beautiful garden. Perhaps it's a healthy body. It could even be well-balanced kids. Ask them how they did it. Usually, they will happily share.

My editor, Karen, reminded me to add a note about giving back to your mentor. That is a good point. When working with a mentor, it is important to give back and pay it forward. You can do this by showing gratitude with a small gift or volunteering time on something important to your mentor. The art of give and take is important.

To thank her sponsor, Lucy became a sponsor to another member of her 12-Step program. In this way, she was paying it forward by volunteering time in an organization that her mentor values.

Gatherings: Humans are social beings. We thrive around other people. This is true of introverts and extroverts alike. We need to socialize in ways that are appropriate for our personality tendencies.

Family gatherings and weekly Al-Anon meetings are Lucy's favorite ways to connect. She and Mitch host a Sunday brunch every other week at their house. It is a great way for their children to pop over and catch up. They extend the invitation to cousins and neighbors as well.

The key for them is to keep it simple. They serve scrambled eggs, bacon, and toast. Guests are welcome to bring their favorite brunch dishes to share. They have cups, forks, and plates on one side of the table. Usually, someone offers to wash the dishes toward the end of the meal.

There is often a lot of chatter and hugs during the bi-monthly event.

During brunch, they learn about how their family members are doing. One day, they all grabbed a glass of orange juice and toasted to their first successful compost. People took turns walking over to see it and congratulate the happy couple.

Whatever community gathering you join, be sure to tell people what you are doing. Celebrate the successes with glasses of orange juice when your compost looks amazing! Share with customers, fellow volunteers, and new friends.

Lucy told Mitch, "We are only as strong as our net." She's right. We all need a well-knit community. And it all starts with one thread.

There are different ways to handle social gatherings.

You may prefer one-on-one time with loved ones. Even so, social gatherings serve a purpose. For the big holiday celebrations, we are creating joint memories to share in later years. It might not be your favorite way to build community, but it's worth stretching your comfort zone from time to time.

It's also important to take proper time for rest after a large social event. Keeping the next day clear of big activities. Scheduling a few hours for nurturing time. Quiet activities like reading a book, lying flat with your legs up the wall, and taking a bath are all nice ways to balance yourself.

We've discussed eight tools in this chapter. They are literature, writing, telephone, service, meditation, prayer, mentorship, and gatherings.

These are the tools that Lucy and many other homesteader mindset friends use. At the end of the chapter, you'll create action steps to incorporate some of them into your life. I've also created a free printable version of this list. You can find it at www.createwellnessproject.com/bookbonus. It's listed under the heading Toolbox.

Now that we've discussed the eight tools for deepening your homesteader mindset. Let's see how Lucy grew her Pocket Puzzle Plan in the next chapter.

EASY-BREEZY END OF CHAPTER TASKS

- Write the eight tools of this chapter on the backside of your Pocket Puzzle Plan.

• Literature	• Meditation
• Telephone	• Prayer
• Writing	• Mentorship
• Service	• Gathering

- Pick two tools and commit to using them this week. One of the chosen tools should involve connecting with another human.
- Call three people to tell them about your Pocket Puzzle Plan. If this seems uncomfortable, do it right now. Pick three people who would love to hear from you. Yes, your mom and your spouse count.

CHAPTER 14

SMALL STEPS LEAD TO GIGANTIC CHANGES

Lucy was aware that changes needed to be made in her personal life. So, she made this one small action at a time.

Farmers' Markets: She started voting with her dollars to promote smaller, sustainable businesses. She began frequenting farmers' markets to buy pesticide-free food and handmade goods. Her favorite part about visiting her local market is her relationships with the vendors. Her baker started selling gluten-free cookies for Lucy's grandson. She merely asked her whether it was possible.

Farmers' markets for the win!

Cloth Bags: Lucy and Mitch switched from plastic bags to cloth bags when shopping. They don't always remember. Sometimes, they forget their bag and load up their arms and pockets to make it back to the car without a bag.

Every time Lucy uses a cloth bag for shopping, she feels a sensation of relief. She is not adding a plastic bag to the landfill. On rare occasions, they need to grab a disposable bag because there isn't another option. Progress, not perfection, is the key.

Their pollution reduction activities came to them gradually and nearly effortlessly. Each new system they incorporate gives them the energy to add a new idea to the mix.

Glass Containers: Lucy buys products in glass containers over products in plastic. She started saving the jars to share leftovers with friends. Soon, their cabinets were full of mason jars for storing food. Through the years, they have slowly etched away at their pollution creation.

Cloth Napkins: Each new step was so tiny it didn't take much effort. There was a stand at the farmers' market that sold cloth napkins. What a great idea! Lucy and Mitch picked out twenty cloth napkins and phased out paper napkins in their kitchen.

Walking: As you know, Lucy lives in a rural part of Pennsylvania. Walking rather than driving the car isn't possible. Right? Wrong. Lucy found a way. Moving her body was essential to staying healthy. Even so, she hated the idea of exercising for the sake of exercising.

So, she habit stacks exercise with errands. Remember her neighbor who barters veggies for chicken eggs every week? That neighbor lives about a fifteen-minute walk from Lucy and Mitch. The couple walks there weekly to swap their goods. It's a great way for Lucy and Mitch to catch up together while getting exercise.

When Lucy goes to town, she usually has two to three errands to run. She makes a day of it by parking at her first errand and walking to all the rest of them. In this way, she easily exercises throughout the day. It also saves on emissions.

She also likes to arrive thirty minutes early for appointments. The extra time is perfect for squeezing in a walk around the block.

Lucy got the idea from Paolo, a friend who lives in the suburbs. Paolo and his wife decided to walk more and save on gas. If anything was less than a half mile from their home, they made the commitment to walk to it. This makes for fun excursions to the coffeehouse and nearby shops.

Chickens: There is another way she utilizes chickens. Live chickens! She saves up a bucket of plant material after weeding and offers it to her neighbor's chickens as a snack. Initially, the chickens were not interested. They were used to eating processed food, but over time, they began to love it. There are bits of protein in the pruned material as well. Chickens love bugs.

Once a season, Lucy invites her neighbor's chickens over for a feast. She sets up a temporary fence around a section of the garden. She lets them scratch, peck, and poop their way through the area. This gently turns the soil and gives the patch natural fertilizer for her next planting.

Goats: Lucy loves the idea of raising a goat for milk. Making goat milk soaps and cheeses seemed like a wonderful idea. However, she and Mitch aren't ready to make the jump into raising a goat. Instead, she offers some of her food scraps to her cousin's goat. She brings over a bucket of leftover rice with fruit peels. Her cousin offers Lucy a bucket of goat poo as fertilizer for the garden. Yet another loop closed.

Natural Fiber Clothing: Mitch gets a kick out of Lucy's compostable shirts. She started shopping for natural fiber clothing. When she buried one of his old cotton shirts in a hole and planted a blueberry bush on top of it, he couldn't help but laugh.

His wife is closing the loop in every way possible and without much fuss. All these years, they kept filling up the trash cans and feeling bad about the waste. He is delighted to see that the joke was on them. Now, they do things differently.

Beeswax Food Wraps: One of Lucy's favorite finds at the local eco-store in town was beeswax food wraps. It troubled her to use plastic wrap when she wanted to pack up her grandchildren's lunches. At first, she didn't think beeswax wrap would work. Luckily, the storekeeper had a sample available and showed Lucy how to wrap food and even bowls with it. It was easy to clean and lasted for months. The best part? Yep, you guessed it. The wraps are compostable.

Bulk Purchases: Lucy found an eco-store during one of her errand day walks. She noticed a store with large bins of grain, nuts, teas, and spices. She visited the store the following week and brought a bag of glass containers. In them, she stores her purchases of rice, rooibos tea, dish soap, and almond butter. Sometimes, she donates a few clean jars for others to use during their shopping, too.

Heat-Resistant Glass Containers: Although Lucy loves using her upcycled mason jars, she found them lacking in some ways. She needed something that she could use for roasting vegetables and freezing leftovers. The most well-known version of heat-resistant glass containers is Pyrex.

A set of Pyrex containers comes with a matching set of reusable plastic lids. Lucy takes her leftovers out of the freezer and allows them to defrost in the fridge. Then she takes off the lid and heats them in the oven. This is not only convenient, but it also gives her family fewer plastic contaminants in their food. The sturdy glassware lasts for decades. The lids last years but do need to be replaced intermittently.

Homemade Household Cleaners: A few months into Lucy's waste reduction, she noticed how stuffed the cabinet under the kitchen sink was. There were plastic bottles for cleaning windows, dish soap, and surface cleaning. You get the picture. Her cabinet was jammed with plastic and chemicals.

It got her thinking. Was there another way? She had already reduced the need for plastic bottles of dish soap by shopping at the bulk store. Lucy was curious. How could she reduce plastic waste while also reducing the chemical load in her household?

Vinegar was her first discovery. It's great for cleaning windows and counter surfaces. That's a two-for-one deal in one easy-to-find ingredient. She put the vinegar in a glass spray bottle and spruced it up with a few drops of essential oils. Lemongrass and rosemary are her personal favorites.

All this vinegar usage got her thinking. How hard would it be to make vinegar from fruit scraps? She found a recipe online and gave it a try using excess lemons from her sister's tree. It took about ten minutes of chopping and thirty seconds of stirring daily to make her very own lemon vinegar.

Are you itching to try your hand at vinegar making? Don't worry. I've included some links on how to do it. You can find it at www.createwellnessproject.com/bookbonus. It's listed under the heading Traditional Food.

Shampoo Bars: This was a big surprise for Lucy. She was convinced that she needed special shampoo to deal with her greasy hair. Mitch suggested they give their local soap vendor's shampoo bar a try. She figured she could deal with a week of greasy hair. What a shock! Her hair was just as manageable and clean as it had been with pricy shampoo. Plus, she liked the look of just two bars: one soap, and one shampoo in the shower. It looked more like a magazine photoshoot than an actual lived-in bathroom.

The beauty of shampoo bars is that you can select ones that have a small ingredient list. Because there is no plastic container, there's no plastic waste. This was an easy change in their bathing routine.

Pallets: Mitch was the first one to bring home a pallet. He saw a few of these wooden transport platforms near a dumpster behind their grocery store. He wasn't sure what he was going to do with them when he brought them home. Lucy had an idea.

Their first pallet project consisted of four pallets. They used old twine from their potting shed to tie the pallets together to make a square box without a top or a bottom. The fourth pallet was tied loosely at one corner so that they could swing that side open like a door. This became their first pallet compost bin. It worked like a charm and took about thirty minutes to build. For a few ideas on building with pallets, you can check out a how-to video at www.createwellnessproject.com/bookbonus under Compost.

Lucy used another set of free pallets to create a potting table in her compost area. She used upcycled nails for that project. It was simple to make, with three pallets forming an open square shape. A piece of discarded plywood became the tabletop. The open side underneath the table is used as storage space for one of her dog poo compost containers.

Thick Curtains: With fuel prices taking a chunk out of their fixed income, Lucy and Mitch came up with inexpensive ways to save. Their living room had a very old window that invited inclement weather into their home. In the summer, it was boiling in the living room. In the winter, there was an icy breeze in the room.

Lucy bought some thick curtains from a thrift store. Mitch hung them on a heavy-duty curtain rod. The curtains provide immediate insulation. In the winter, they keep the curtains closed during the early morning and evening hours. When open, the sun warms the room and keeps the heat captured in the room as the temperature drops.

On summer days, they keep the windows open in the early morning hours to let the fresh air into the house. Before the sun heats up the room, they close the curtains. They leave the room shaded and cool throughout the day. The curtains alone make a huge difference in the summer. The living room is often the coolest room in the house without an air conditioner.

Limit Consumption: Lucy didn't know that a minimalist lifestyle was a thing. All she knew was that she was tired of being told that buying a select five hundred items every day would make her happy. Believe me, she tried. Shopping had once been a hobby for her and her daughter. When she was working, she would visit the mall (and later online) to browse for things that her family might need.

It was the unnecessary products that bugged her. A bit of advertising would sink into her head. She would be convinced that this item, which she had never needed before, would make her life better. She felt a tiny blip of joy as she brought the item home or opened the package in her kitchen.

And as quick as that, the bliss faded. Lucy was stuck with the problem of where to fit this clunky thing in her cupboards. Two more weeks would go by, and she'd start feeling guilty for not using it. Two years of dust, and she would avoid the cupboard where she placed it. The momentary blip of joy ended up costing her a wad of money, a feeling of clutter, and a lot of resentment.

Consumerism can be described as the idea that having is more important than being.

As Lucy continued her waste reduction, her habit of buying useless things diminished. A by-product of looking at the waste she was creating was that she had no desire to buy more clutter. Her life is fulfilling with the new connections she is making. The closed loops she is creating satisfied her need for more.

She inadvertently reduced the urge to buy things in order to be happier because she is happier.

In this chapter, you can see how Lucy took the puzzle plan corner of "reduce waste" and made it a priority in her life. She started by merely thinking about it and then letting the desire go. In this way, she told her brain that this was an important topic and allowed her subconscious to work on it. The insight that popped up here and there was a result of making the "reduce waste" theme a priority in her life.

When insight struck her, Lucy was delighted. She took action with small ideas like picking up litter at the park. She immersed herself in the world of clean living by talking to her friends and family about it. Mitch was happy to be a part of her green team.

Lucy signed up for an eco-friendly newsletter. She found it while watching videos on making vinegar and upcycling glass containers. Oftentimes, the newsletter would suggest a book to read or a video to watch. Mitch and Lucy would sit together with cups of tea and watch others who were living green lives.

Just as you are reading this chapter and ideas are popping up for you, Lucy was inspired. The changes others were making in their life gave her inspiration. She knows that slow and steady is the pace that works for her. Lucy is at a unique time in her life. She recognizes how precious life is but has no desire to rush through it.

She rushed through much of her childhood and young adult life. Trying to keep up with the expectations of others. She practically sprinted through her twenties in an attempt to prove herself worthy. It wasn't until retirement age that she made an active decision to stop running from the present moment. She allowed herself to be content with an aging body, a messy garden, and a sagging house.

Without the help of magazines, she loved her body as is. She thanked it each day for getting her out of bed. Her garden was messy. It was also beloved by her and provided adventurous strolls for her grandchildren. The children won't remember the weeds here and there. But they will have memories of picking fresh berries for their pancakes with Grandpa. And the sagging house? It's such a gift to have a house at all. Sagging added character.

Comparison isn't an issue for her. Instead, she is inspired and curious. Perhaps, you can take that tip with you into your homesteader mindset. Even if you're younger than Lucy, now is the perfect time to be at ease with yourself.

EASY-BREEZY END OF CHAPTER TASKS

- Once you have finished your first corner, revise the Pocket Puzzle Plan with a new puzzle piece.
  - Review your chapter ten list in your Homesteader Mindset Journal for ideas.
  - If you're still knee-deep in your first corner, stay there. Enjoy the process.
    - Start daydreaming about the next corner.
    - Give yourself three mini-goals to accomplish before moving on to the next corner.

- Here are three mini-goals that Lucy made:
  - Swap paper napkins for cloth napkins.
  - Buy in bulk using reusable glass containers.
  - Create an easy compost system for her fruit and vegetable scraps.

- Take a moment to congratulate yourself for reading this book. You can check that task off your list. Mini-celebrations motivate us to continue the path.
- Consider three ways that you can discuss the topics in this book with others. Write those ideas down and take action one corner at a time.

CHAPTER 15:

A LITTLE MORE HOMESTEADER MINDSET

We made it. Unless you're in the bookstore flipping to the back page, you walked with me through this entire book. No judgment on the back page peekers. I do that all the time. If only I could have flipped to the back page of my relationships in early adulthood. That would have saved me quite a few nights of chocolate chip cookie dough and tears.

For those of you who are finishing this book on your first read through, well done. Perhaps the examples you read will save you a few nights of angst. There still might be cookie dough moments in your future, but it will be sprinkled with hope. The kind of optimism that holds up your spoon to the heavens and declares, "If Tamara (or Lucy and Mitch or Sara and Jim) can do it, so can I!"

Your time is precious. It is a great honor that you choose to bookmark some of it and learn about the many ways of creating a homesteader mindset. And boy, oh boy, there are many paths. Let's quickly summarize the important tips here.

CHANGE IS POSSIBLE FOR EVERYONE

In part one, five characters showed examples of massive change. Single twentysomething working poor. Middle-class couple with school-age children. Retirement-age couple with fixed income.

Although you may not fall neatly into one of these groups, each character has something of value to share. Mindset shifts and tiny habit changes can lead to grand awakenings. A homesteader mindset is often just around the corner of one small action.

SIMPLE ACTIONS CAN CHANGE YOUR LIFE

In part two, we delved into three mindset shifts needed to create a homesteader mindset. We learned how to play and create more in our lives. We looked at the power of learning new things to feed our curious nature. And we closed the loop with actionable items you can do right now to change your life.

KICKING OUTDATED IDEAS TO THE CURB

In part three, we deconstructed three major myths that get people stuck. We unstuck ourselves by finding time that we didn't know was there. We identified ways to make changes on the cheap. Lastly, we learned to keep things simple. The smallest changes in routine can create massive improvements in our lives.

POCKET PUZZLE PLAN TO THE RESCUE!

In part four, we introduced the three-step process called the Pocket Puzzle Plan. The PIP method starts with the tiny step of picking (P) your puzzle corner. Then you work your way from easy to successful. From there, we move to step two, which is daily immersion (I) during found time. Lastly, you take the wins from steps one and two to make your homesteader mindset a priority (P).

As human beings, we all crave connection. The trick is to make it important. Find the corners that you wish to work on first. Undistracted alone time is lacking for many of us. Maybe you start there. A little connection to self goes a long way.

Be okay with messy. Do things imperfectly. Perfectly imperfect is way cooler in the long run.

Here are a few stumbling blocks and solutions that can help.

What if. . .

. . .you don't know where to start.

Analysis paralysis can happen to the best of us. Take it s-l-o-w. Commit to a one-minute change in your daily routine. If you don't know what to do during the sixty-second commitment, take a pen and highlighter. Reread this book from the start. Underline sentences that move you. Highlight things you want to remember. Make a to-try list on one of the first few pages of the book. Take a long slow breath. You've got this!

. . . you feel overwhelmed.

Start by moving your body for two minutes. Walk in place. Put on a song and dance. Move some of that stuck energy in your system. Then, review the tools in chapter thirteen. Start your self-care practice using these tools before you head into other changes.

. . . you feel alone.

You may not be currently surrounded by people who are interested in a homesteader mindset. That doesn't mean they don't exist. Joining a homesteader mailing list will connect you with more of us. I share events and updates with my circle via a monthly newsletter.

In-person gatherings are important, too. Tamara found her community through volunteering. Sara and Jim found theirs through church and accepting help. Lucy and Mitch are active in 12-Step groups and their extended family. My husband and I visit permaculture farms and traditional food gatherings. Growing our community is a priority. And it makes travel more fun when you have friends to visit now and then.

These are only a few options for discovering your community. Some groups are formed around hobbies like self-defense classes or beach clean-up days. Think about what is important to you and join that team.

It's a great idea to get out there and meet fellow humans in person. Revisit the section on gatherings in chapter thirteen. What I know for sure is that you are not the only person who bought this book. There are a ton of homesteader mindset peeps floating around this beautiful globe. And they are looking for a friend just like you.

It has been a gift to share nuggets of gold with you. I'm grateful for your brave, curious, adventurous spirit. Now get out there and have a beautiful life with your homesteader mindset. You deserve it.

May you be happy. May you be peaceful. May you be free, free, free.

PROMISED RECIPES

GARDEN HERBAL INFUSION
FROM CHAPTER ONE

Garden herbal infusion (GHI) is a fancy term for the infused water that I drink daily. I often offer it at our parties. The infusion needed a name to differentiate it from the still water in the pitcher next to it. I usually need to refill the GHI pitcher five times more than the still water during our gatherings. Why? Because it's refreshing and delicious. Our bodies know what's good for us.

Every couple of days, I go out to my garden and make a GHI for my family. It's an easy, enjoyable practice. The recipe is similar to the recipes of Louisiana rootworkers in one way. You use what you have handy and what calls to you.

Another American herb expert calls it simpling. She would go into her garden and ask herself and the garden what was needed that day. Simpling is also known as a European medieval practice of healing with one herb at a time. But that's not what the American herb expert was referring to. So, I use her definition when I forage in my garden.

Prep: 5 minutes   Cook: 10 minutes

INGREDIENTS

Three or more herbs from your garden. If you don't have a garden yet, pick three to four herbs from the farmers' market or grocery store. Here is a list of herbs I use on a regular basis.

• basil	• rosemary	• lemongrass
• thyme	• lemon balm	• oregano
• lavender	• sage	• marigold
• calendula	• peppermint	• spearmint
• ginger	• chrysanthemum	• mallow

INSTRUCTIONS

- Gather a handful of fresh herbs. Treat the selection process as meditation.
  - If you are foraging in your garden, ask yourself what calls to you. Snip off one herb and hold it next to another herb to smell their fragrances together. If you like the combination, choose those for your infusion. I choose three or more for mine.
  - If selecting herbs at the store or farmers' market, smell them together as well.

- Bring 24 ounces of water to a boil. The amount doesn't matter. Boil enough to fill a pitcher.
- While the water is boiling, rinse the herbs in lukewarm water.
- Place the herbs into the pitcher.
- Add the hot water.
- Let it steep for 5 to 10 minutes before serving.

I leave the infusion on my counter and drink it throughout the day. In the afternoon, I put it in the refrigerator. Depending on the herbs, I can sometimes make a second or third infusion.

You can also make a cold brew version with room temperature water. That takes a few hours to flavor but works great in the summer.

A FEW TIPS

Use minty herbs in the warm seasons. They are too cool for your body in the cold seasons. This is based on traditional Chinese medicine.

Thyme is the taste bully of my herb collection. Use it sparingly or it will out-flavor everything else.

Ginger is a wonderful herb. It's great for colds, flu, and digestive issues.

(I could write an entire book on the healing properties of herbs. In fact, I will. One upcoming book in *The Homesteader Mindset* series will focus on medicine from your kitchen and garden. So, keep your eye out for that.)

You will need a pitcher. I prefer a jumbo mason jar with a removable pour spout lid. I buy my tops from a company called MasonTops.com. Go figure! If I don't have a lid, I stuff a cloth napkin into the top as a makeshift cover. A cloth lid works for parties.

HONEY BAKED PEARS

FROM CHAPTER SIX

When we're invited to a potluck and I want to be fancy, I make this dessert. It's so easy. You know how some recipes say it's five minutes of prep time, but it's really fifty minutes? Thankfully, this is not one of those. It's magazine pretty which makes people think I spent close to an hour designing this impeccable dish.

The best step-by-step recipe for honey baked pears comes from skinnytaste.com. Because it's copyright protected, I cannot print it, but I can share their link. They offer a ton of yummy big batch freezer meals, too.

www.skinnytaste.com/baked-pears-with-walnuts-and-honey

The recipe calls for walnuts. You can use any nuts you have on hand. Crushed nuts perish quicker and are more expensive. I use a mortar and pestle to crush nuts. You could also wrap a handful of whole nuts in a clean kitchen towel and smash them down with a large ladle.

If you intend on wowing dinner guests, saunter into the dining area with baked honey pears. It gets a standing ovation every time. Okay, maybe not an actual standing ovation as that would be a strange occurrence over dinner. But you get my drift.

APPLE COMPOTE RECIPE
FROM CHAPTER NINE

Apple compote has many purposes. It can be used as a naturally sweet, naturally refined sugar-free jam on nut butter sandwiches. It can be topped with whipped cream to enjoy as a dessert. It's a great way to boost the body with healing herbs like cinnamon.

In Chinese herbology, cinnamon is a wonder herb. It aids digestion, warms up the meridians and even helps improve your mood. There are studies that show cinnamon helps regulate blood sugar.

The difference between apple compote and applesauce is consistency. Applesauce is pureed whereas apple compote still has soft chunks of cooked apple in it. For me, blending up compote into a sauce is one extra step. I am all about easy home cooking. So, it's apple compote for my house!

This recipe is an adaptation from an applesauce recipe that I found AllRecipes.com. In their slower cooker cider applesauce recipe, they recommend peeled apples. Again, that's not going to happen in my kitchen.

Firstly, it's an additional step, and you know how I feel about that. Secondly, edible peels contain nutrients that I'm interested in eating. The cores go into the compost. The peels go into our bellies.

Prep: 10 minutes   Cook: 2–3 hours

INGREDIENTS

- 5–7 apples, cored and cut into one-inch chunks
  - *I use a small 1.5 quart slow cooker.*

- 1 tablespoon ground cinnamon
  - *You can start with half the spices to be safe. After a few preparations, you'll be able to eyeball the amounts.*

- ½ teaspoon ground cloves
  - *Use allspice as a substitute.*

- ¼ teaspoon ground nutmeg
  - *Skip this spice if you don't have it. Cinnamon is the only must have for this recipe.*

INSTRUCTIONS

- Add apple chunks to your slower cooker. Sprinkle the spices over the apples.
- Cook on High for 2 to 3 hours.
- Stir lazily. If it looks like mushy goodness, it's done.

A WORD ABOUT SLOW COOKERS

We have two small 1.5-quart slow cookers because we use them so much. They are perfect for rice, overnight oatmeal, and afternoon compote. They are easy to handle for cleaning.

We also have an eight-quart slow cooker that we use weekly for large batch meals like soup, chili, and casseroles. That beast is harder to clean because it's heavy, but it helps us when doubling recipes. We freeze the extra servings as our version of fast food.

For me, a slow cooker is the best investment to make when first learning how to cook. And when learning how to fit cooking into your busy schedule. At the time of writing this, a small slow cooker cost $12.

When I first started cooking, I went online and picked two simple recipes to try. I'm talking chop-up-three-things-add-spice simple. I am the queen of easy batch cooking. And it works for us.

SMALL REQUEST

I know. I know.

I don't want it to be over either. It's such fun to share excitement with friends like you.

If you enjoyed this book, would you do me a favor?

Would you please offer an honest review on Amazon, Goodreads and where you bought this book?

Reviews are extremely important for self-published authors. Here's why.

- Your review will help other readers find this itty-bitty book in the vast ocean of online bookshops.

- By writing a review, you are supporting an artist. The more you help artists, the more artists can create art. For me, art comes in the form of this book. My notebook doodles are cute, but they won't be showcased in the Louvre anytime soon.

- Offering a helpful review feels good. It's easy to digest vitamin G. And I don't mean riboflavin. I mean G for gratitude.

I sure did get my shot of gratitude writing this book for you. And my thanks continue.

GRATITUDE

This is the easiest and hardest part of the book to write. Easiest because I have so many amazing people to thank. Hardest because I could fill a whole other book with this section alone. I have an abundance of angels and heroes in my life.

To my husband, Chris—there is not a day that goes by where I do not marvel at the exceptional man I married. Thank you for continuing to grow in life and in love. Your unwavering faith in me is astounding.

To Eli—I'm exceptionally lucky to have you in my life. What a lovely human you are! Our letters are some of my favorite moments.

To my Thursday night gals—I thank each and every one of you for talking me off the cliff more than once. Your enthusiasm for my work has been an incredible support.

To Dunya, Amanda, Jennifer, Pammie, Emma, and Maggie—I'm grateful for your endless curiosity and kindness around my writing journey. Your encouragement has been a sanity saver.

To my parents, Joseph and Valentina, and my sea of siblings, in-laws, nieces, and nephews—I appreciate your generosity and kindness.

To the wonderful individuals who helped make this book a possibility— my compassionate editor, Karen Hunsanger; my inspiring cover and interior designer, Dino Marino; my sharp-eyed proofreader, Catherine Turner; and my book coach extraordinaire, Honorée Corder.

To my readers—I am especially grateful for you.

ABOUT THE AUTHOR

Elizabeth Bruckner is a world wanderer, acupuncturist, and rescue dog lover. In 2020, she started growing her own food in the suburbs of Los Angeles. Through research and experimentation, she taught herself to repair soil, compost kitchen scraps, ferment like an alchemist, harvest crops, cook traditional food, and live a life that is more connected than she ever thought possible.

She holds a Master of Science in Acupuncture and Oriental Medicine. Her area of expertise at Green Jade Acupuncture is mental health. She focuses her skills on helping people recover from anxiety, depression, burnout, and other stress-related ailments through treatment and habit creation.

You can find out more at www.createwellnessproject.com.